10 scriptures to get you through high school

D1236946

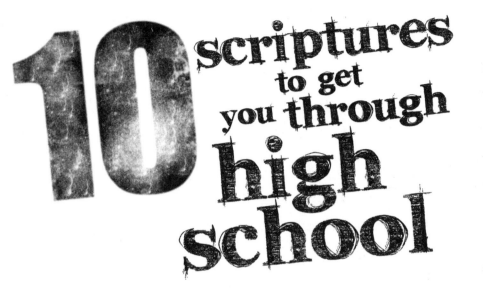

10 scriptures to get you through high school

shad martin

CFI

AN IMPRINT OF CEDAR FORT, INC.

Springville, Utah

© 2012 Shad Martin

All rights reserved.

No part of this book may be reproduced in any form whatsoever, whether by graphic, visual, electronic, film, microfilm, tape recording, or any other means, without prior written permission of the publisher, except in the case of brief passages embodied in critical reviews and articles.

This is not an official publication of The Church of Jesus Christ of Latter-day Saints. The opinions and views expressed herein belong solely to the author and do not necessarily represent the opinions or views of Cedar Fort, Inc. Permission for the use of sources, graphics, and photos is also solely the responsibility of the author.

ISBN 13: 978-1-4621-1039-1

Published by CFI, an imprint of Cedar Fort, Inc., 2373 W. 700 S., Springville, UT 84663
Distributed by Cedar Fort, Inc., www.cedarfort.com

LIBRARY OF CONGRESS CATALOGING-IN-PUBLICATION DATA

Martin, Shad, 1976- author.
  10 scriptures to get you through high school / Shad Martin.
     pages cm
  ISBN 978-1-4621-1039-1 (alk. paper)
  1. Christian life--Mormon authors. 2. Mormon youth--Religious life. I.
Title. II. Title: Ten scriptures to get you through high school.

  BX8656.M348 2012
  248.8'3--dc23

                              2012015653

Cover design by Brian Halley
Cover design © 2012 by Lyle Mortimer
Edited and typeset by Kelley Konzak

Printed in the United States of America

10 9 8 7 6 5 4 3 2 1

Printed on acid-free paper

I want to dedicate this book to my wonderful nieces and nephews, and especially to my three beautiful daughters, Emma, Isabella, and Clara. I wrote this book with you in my mind and heart. I love you guys so much. My prayer is that this book will help someone. If it helps one person come closer to the Savior, it will be worth the effort.

contents

acknowledgments

I AM grateful for Cedar Fort Publishing, who approached me and gave me this opportunity to share my testimony. I am grateful for my parents and grandparents and many family members who instilled in me a love for the principles within this book. I am especially grateful for my wife, Robin, who supports me in so many ways, allows me to do the things that I love, and has made many sacrifices in order for me to do so.

introduction

it is written

I WOULD like to start this book by giving you a warning. I give this warning because of a pattern I began to recognize as I studied my scriptures. Here it is:

When something spiritually significant is about to happen in your life, Satan will often do all he can to prevent it from happening.

Here are three accounts from the scriptures where I believe this pattern is clearly seen.

Number one: The prophet Joseph Smith was a teenager when he was confused about the many different ideas being taught about religion. He picked up the bible and read James 1:5, which teaches, "If any of you lack wisdom, let him ask of God, that giveth to all men liberally, and upbraideth not; and it shall be given him." This scripture had a powerful effect upon him, and he decided to do just as James had directed. He walked into a grove of trees, knelt down, and began to pray with all his heart. The dark night of the Apostasy was just seconds from giving way to the dawn of the Restoration.

As he knelt to pray, he was immediately seized upon

by some power of the adversary, which entirely over-
came him and bound his tongue so that he could not
speak. Thick darkness gathered around him, and he
thought he was doomed to sudden destruction.

Why would Satan come to Joseph Smith, a fourteen-
year-old farm boy, and try to prevent him from uttering
that all-important prayer? I think the answer is obvious.
He was trying to prevent one of the most pivotal events in
the history of the world from happening. He was trying
to prevent the First Vision and the Restoration that followed. But Joseph called upon God, and God and Jesus
Christ appeared to him and spoke, giving him instructions and direction that would change the world forever.

This pattern of Satan trying to prevent great things
from happening is laced throughout the scriptures.

Number two: The scriptures tell us that Moses was
visited by God and that God told him he had a work for
him to do. What work was that? Among other things,
Moses was going to help deliver the children of Israel,
who had not been able to worship the Lord as they
pleased for many, many years, from hundreds of years
of Egyptian bondage. Freedom was just on the horizon.

As Moses sat regaining his strength and contem-
plating what had just happened to him, the scriptures
record that Satan came tempting him, saying: "Moses,
son of man, worship me" (Moses 1:12). Moses had to
command Satan to depart three times before he finally
had a temper tantrum and fled.

After Satan had departed, "Moses lifted up his eyes
unto heaven. . . . And calling upon the name of God,
he beheld his glory again." On this occasion God told
Moses that he would be made "stronger than many
waters; for they shall obey thy command as if thou wert

God. And lo, I am with thee, even unto the end of thy days; for thou shalt deliver my people from bondage" (Moses 1:24–26).

Why did Satan appear to Moses? Something awesome was about to happen. Satan loved the fact that God's chosen people were in bondage to the Egyptians and therefore could not worship God as they pleased. Satan was trying to prevent the deliverance of the children of Israel.

Number three: Jesus Christ went down into the water to be baptized of John and then went up into a mountain to be with God and to fast and pray for forty days and forty nights preparing for his mortal ministry. While he was on the mountain, Satan came three times tempting him: first, to turn stones to bread; second, to jump off a cliff to see if angels really would save him; and third, to worship Satan, for which he would supposedly get all the kingdoms and glory of the world (Matthew 4:1–11; see footnotes for Joseph Smith Translation). Jesus did not give in to these temptations and went on to teach, bless, heal, and atone for all of mankind.

Why did Satan come to the Son of God on the eve of his mortal ministry? The most wonderful and significant event that was ever going to occur in human history was about to take place, and he wanted to stop it. If he could stop the Savior before he even got started, imagine the effect that could have had on the rest of human history.

These three stories expose Satan. In each one he is found trying to prevent something wonderful and eternally significant from occurring. So what does this have to do with you as a teenager? Here you sit, reading this book, with so many wonderful and eternally important events just on the horizon of *your* life. The temple, the Melchizedek Priesthood, missions, marriages, motherhood and fatherhood, and the list goes on. We should not act as though the adversary is going to stand idly by and hope we make bad decisions. The pattern above suggests otherwise. President Gordon B. Hinckley said that the youth of the Church are "particular targets for the adversary." He went on to explain that if Satan "can get you now, he knows he may win you for a lifetime."[1]

There may be no time in life fraught with more temptation than the teenage years. In one of his first conference addresses as president of the Church, President Monson said, "Our youth, our precious youth, in particular, face temptations we can scarcely comprehend."[2] You are growing up in a world that calls "evil good and good evil" (Isaiah 5:20). You are bombarded daily with flashing images enticing you to do things that are contrary to the commandments. But there is hope and help. As with everything, the Savior Jesus Christ is our perfect example. When He was on the mountain and Satan came tempting Him, he responded each time with the phrase "It is written" and then quoted a scripture that exposed Satan's temptation as a lie.

This book is designed to arm you with ten scriptures that teach true doctrines dealing with some of the more common temptations that the adversary will bombard you with during your high school years.

1. The temptation to continue hanging out with a friend or group of friends even if they are a bad influence on you.
2. The temptation to think the Church is restrictive and that life would be so much more fun without all of the Church's rules.

3. The temptation to do something that you know is wrong to fit in with or to impress someone else.
4. The temptation to not say your prayers, either out of laziness or because you feel guilty for something you have done.
5. The temptation to not like yourself and wish you were somebody else.
6. The temptation to feel that God must not care about you because of the trials you are experiencing.
7. The temptation to live for today with no regard for tomorrow or eternity.
8. The temptation to focus so much on yourself and on making yourself look good that you become self-centered and inconsiderate of others.
9. The temptation to do so many good things that the most important things fall out of your life.
10. The temptation to hide your sins because you are afraid or embarrassed to confess them.

Countless scriptures provide us with guidance and direction. It is my prayer that after becoming more familiar with the ten scriptures in this book you will be able to draw strength from them to resist the temptations of the adversary. I hope that you will be able to respond to the adversary as Jesus did when he said "It is written" and then quoted scriptures that strengthened him. When you do so, I know you will be able to experience all the wonderful and eternally significant events that are just on the horizon of your lives.

Notes

1. Gordon B. Hinckley, "Loyalty," *Ensign*, May 2003, 58.
2. Thomas S. Monson, "Looking Back and Moving Forward," *Ensign*, May 2008, 87–90.

matthew 18:8-9 (jst)

TEMPTATION

To continue hanging out with a friend or group of friends even if they are a bad influence on you.

IT IS WRITTEN

Wherefore if thy hand or thy foot offend thee, cut them off, and cast them from thee: it is better for thee to enter into life halt or maimed, rather than having two hands or two feet to be cast into everlasting fire.

And if thine eye offend thee, pluck it out, and cast it from thee: it is better for thee to enter into life with one eye, rather than having two eyes to be cast into hell fire. And a man's hand is his friend, and his foot, also; and a man's eye, are they of his own household. (See footnote a in verse 9.)

THE word *offend* in this verse could also be translated "causes you to sin" or "causes you to stumble." I believe the Savior is saying that if your friends are causing you to sin or stumble, then you should cut them off from your life.

Anyone who has ever had to do this knows how tough and awkward this can be. It is important to recognize what is implied by the analogy the Savior uses. I think there is a reason the Savior did not say, "And if the weed does not look good in your garden, pick it." He used the plucking of eyes and the cutting off of limbs for a reason. I cannot imagine how painful it would be to gouge out my own eye or to cut off my hand or foot. I think he knows how painful it is to leave a friend or a group of friends even though they may be a destructive influence on us. Anyone who has had to say good-bye to a friend or a group of friends knows the pains and fears associated with doing so. Who am I going to hang out with at lunch, at the football game, or after school? How awkward is it going to be to tell them why I am not hanging out with them anymore? These questions cause a lot of concern and anxiety, and in the face of these questions, some of you may shy away from doing what you know you should do. But the Savior's point is clear: it is better to go to heaven without an eye or hand or foot than it is to go to hell with those things. Likewise it is better to go to heaven after cutting off a friend from your life than it is to go to hell with them.

One time I asked a group of teenagers why they think the Savior used the analogy of cutting off hands or feet or plucking out an eye to represent saying good-bye to a friend. Their answers highlighted for me how tough it can be for a young person to make this decision. One said, "I think he used that analogy because your friends become part of you." Another said, "I think he used that analogy because, just like cutting off an arm or a foot or plucking out an eye, when you cut off certain friends, you won't be able to do some of the things you did before."

A couple of scripture stories speak to the importance of saying good-bye to a friend who is trying to "cause you to stumble," even when it is tough.

Many of you are familiar with the story of Samson and Delilah in Judges 16. Samson was a very strong man, and the Philistines became curious about the source of his great strength. In actuality, they wanted to know how they could make him lose his strength because he had been such a nuisance to them. At the same time, Samson had become infatuated with a lady named Delilah.

The Philistines came to Delilah and offered her a fortune in silver if she could find out the source of Samson's great strength. She went to Samson and asked him to tell her. Samson must have had a little bit of a premonition that she was up to no good because he lied to her and told her that if she were to tie him up with "seven green withs [new cords; for example, fresh or moist sinews from animals]," then he would lose his strength and "be as another man." Eventually he fell asleep and woke up all tied up in seven green withs. The Philistines were waiting in the chamber for him to wake up so that they could pounce on him. When Delilah woke him up telling him the "Philistines be upon thee," Samson arose, easily snapped the withs, and chased off the frustrated Philistines.

Delilah got mad at Samson and told him that he had mocked her and told her lies. She then begged him to tell her the source of his great strength. He replied in essence, "Okay, okay. If they bind me with new ropes that have never tied up anyone else, then I will lose my strength." Eventually he fell asleep, and once again Delilah tied him up, this time with new ropes, and yelled, "the Philistines be upon thee." Samson once again woke up, broke the ropes like a thread, and chased off the Philistines.

Delilah was very upset and accused Samson of mocking her. She begged him again to tell her the source of his strength. He told her that if she were to weave his seven locks together, he would be made weak. He once again woke up with all his strength. That was when Delilah pulled out the big guns.

"How canst thou say, I love thee, when thine heart is not with me? thou hast mocked me these three times, and hast not told me wherein thy great strength lieth." The scriptures say that she "pressed him daily with her words, and urged him."

Finally Samson gave in to the press. Though it was obvious that Delilah's goal was to weaken him, he told her that if she were to shave his head with a razor, he would be made weak. Samson was a Nazarite, and the Nazarite code prohibited him from cutting his hair. The Nazarite covenant was the source of Samson's strength. When Samson woke up with his head shaved, his strength was gone, but he did not know it. Tragically, the Philistines took him, put out his eyes, and caused him to be a slave. His life ended when his hair grew back and he received enough strength to knock down two pillars, making a house fall on him and on those who had gathered to mock him.

What a sad story. It is almost frustrating to read. When I read it, I want to say, "Samson! What is wrong with you? How could you be so dense?"

Well, what is done is done as far as Samson goes, but what about you? When would you have said good-bye to Delilah? I think that Samson should have said good-bye when it became obvious that her intent was to make him weak by getting him to break his Nazarite code.

Like Samson, you have a code given to you that is intended to make you strong. As a matter of fact, it is called the *For the Strength of Youth* pamphlet. If there is someone in your life who "presses upon you daily" to break the "code" within *For the Strength of Youth*, you should be smarter than Samson was and say good-bye. Will it be tough? Yes, of course it will be tough. But it will not be as tough as dealing with the consequences of giving in to their press. Just ask Samson.

Another sad story, this one from the Book of Mormon, illustrates why it is so important to surround yourself with the right kind of people. In Mosiah, chapter eleven, Noah had the kingdom conferred upon him after the death of his father, Zeniff. One of the first things that Noah did was "put down all of the priests that had been consecrated by his father, and consecrated new ones in their stead, such as were lifted up in the pride of their hearts." By so doing, the scriptures read, he and they were "supported in their laziness and in their idolatry, and in their whoredoms." I wonder why Noah did what he did. Why would he put down the good priests who had worked alongside his father and appoint new ones? I think the answer is obvious. He wanted to surround himself with people who would allow him to be lazy and immoral without nagging him about it all the time.

This decision eventually led to Noah's major downfall. Because of the wickedness of King Noah and his people, the Lord sent the prophet Abinadi to preach to them and to call them to repentance. At the conclusion of

Abinadi's moving warning, the scriptures record, Noah was about to release Abinadi. "But the priests lifted up their voices against him, . . . saying: He has reviled the king. Therefore the king was stirred up in anger against him, and he delivered him up that he might be slain" (Mosiah 17:12). What a tragedy. I have often wondered how the story would have ended if Noah had chosen better friends. If his friends would have said something like, "I don't feel like it is right to kill him. Let's let him go. Let's do what is right," this story might have been one of those beloved Book of Mormon stories where we see someone undergo a mighty change of heart.

Unfortunately King Noah had surrounded himself with people who persuaded him to do wrong. When a critical decision came into his life, he was not willing to say good-bye to them, and he went down with them. Eventually his life ended when he was put to death by fire, just as Abinadi had prophesied.

On the other hand, one of King Noah's friends was brave enough to leave his associates and do what he knew was right. Alma listened to Abinadi and made the hard decision to cut himself off from his former friends. Did life get easy for Alma after? No. He was in hiding for a while, and one of his former fellow priests was instrumental in putting him into bondage. I am sure it was not easy for Alma. But eventually he went on to be one of the greatest and most beloved of all the Book of Mormon prophets and to change the whole history of the Book of Mormon.

As I mentioned before, the Savior knows that it is hard to say good-bye to a good friend. He knows it will hurt. I believe that is why he used the analogy he did. But it is better to cut a friend off than it is to follow him down to the bad consequences that always accompany sin.

There is another important item to talk about when speaking of this scripture. I don't think the Savior wants us to kick everyone out of our life as soon as they make a mistake. We all make mistakes. I think we should first strive to persuade our errant friend to choose the right. I think that is what a true friend does. In speaking with youth and asking them what a true friend is, many times they will say, "Someone who lets me be me." Well, that is great unless the "you" you are being is not the best "you" you can be. By standing up to a friend and saying, "We should not do this. We know it is wrong," you might not only save yourself but also save your friend from being "cast into hell fire."

You will recall that before Nephi left his older brothers, he pled with them to keep the commandments, prayed for them, asked them to pray, shared with them the spiritual experiences he had, and forgave them on many occasions. We should do the same.

There is a caution to mention here though. Sometimes people think they have to be part of a bad crowd in order to be a positive influence in their lives. A great friend of mine has some sisters who kept getting themselves into trouble by trying to "save" young men who were on the wrong track. I think he gave them great advice. He told them to maintain "home court advantage." What he meant by this was that his sisters should not feel like they had to participate in the bad things the boys were doing if they were going to affect their lives. They should invite the boys to good, wholesome, and safe environments. Invite them to mutual, to family home evening, or on a group date or activity with a bunch of great kids. In other words, you stay on higher ground and invite them up; you don't go to dangerous places to rescue them. I think this is wise counsel.

One of the best friends in all of scripture is a donkey. That's right, a donkey. In Numbers 22 a man named Balak, king of the Moabites, was afraid of the Israelite armies because of how successful they had been against the armies of the Amorites. He was afraid that Israel was going to come upon his people. Out of fear, Balak sent men to Balaam, a prophet in Israel, asking him to come to Moab and use his priesthood power to curse the armies of Israel. Balak offered Balaam money and cattle to do so. Balaam asked God, and God obviously told him no.

Balak then sent even more important men to Balaam with even more riches. Balaam responded with, "If Balak would give me his house full of silver and gold, I cannot go beyond the word of the Lord." In other words, I cannot use God's power in a way that he does not want me to.

Against wise judgment, Balaam decided to meet with the king of Moab anyway. He saddled up his donkey and began the trip. Suddenly the donkey turned and attempted to go another way. This angered Balaam, and he hit his donkey. He tried to resume the journey toward Moab, but the donkey thrust herself against a nearby wall, crushing Balaam's foot, and he hit her again. He tried to get her to continue toward Moab, but this time the donkey just fell to the ground and refused to move. Filled with rage and anger, Balaam picked up his staff and struck the donkey.

What happened next is something that I would love to see if we are permitted in the next life to go back and look upon events that occurred here on earth. The Lord opened the mouth of the donkey, and the donkey spoke to Balaam, saying, "What have I done unto thee, that thou hast smitten me these three times?" Can you imagine what was going through Balaam's mind when his donkey started to talk to him? Balaam tells the donkey that he wishes he had a sword to kill her because she had "mocked" him three times. The donkey asked Balaam if she had ever disobeyed him before. And then the Lord opened Balaam's eyes and revealed to him what was the matter with his donkey. There, standing before him, was a destroying angel with his sword drawn, ready to kill Balaam. The angel then tells Balaam that if it were not for his donkey, he would have been slain.

Every now and then, you will need to be like the donkey and dig in your heels and do all you can to keep your friends from walking into the path of destroying angels. Your friends might lash out at you, call you names, and threaten to leave you like Balaam did to his donkey. But a great friend will not watch someone they love walk into the sword of a destroying angel without trying to do something. You need to do all you can to save yourself and your friends from the adversary and his angels who are all around us. Don't let your friends leave for "Moab" without saying anything. If they ultimately decide to go despite your warnings, for heaven's sake, do not go with them. Don't follow your friends to "Moab."

I hope that the next time you are faced with the tempting, awkward, and painful situation where a friend is trying to persuade you to stumble and lose your strength, you will have the courage to be an Alma and not a Samson or Noah. May you be like Balaam's donkey and not only do what's right yourself but try to help your friend do what is right as well. May you remember what is written in Matthew 18:8–9:

> Wherefore if thy hand or thy foot offend thee, cut them off, and cast them from thee: it is better for thee to enter into life halt or maimed, rather than having two hands or two feet to be cast into everlasting fire.
>
> And if thine eye offend thee, pluck it out, and cast it from thee: it is better for thee to enter into life with one eye, rather than having two eyes to be cast into hell fire. And a man's hand is his friend, and his foot, also; and a man's eye, are they of his own household. (See footnote a in verse 9.)

2 mosiah 2:41

TEMPTATION

To think the Church is restrictive and that life would be so much more fun without all of the Church's rules.

IT IS WRITTEN

And moreover, I would desire that ye should consider on the blessed and happy state of those that keep the commandments of God. For behold, they are blessed in all things, both temporal and spiritual; and if they hold out faithful to the end they are received into heaven, that thereby they may dwell with God in a state of never-ending happiness. O remember, remember that these things are true; for the Lord God hath spoken it.

SATAN is good at what he does and is skilled at making sin look fun, exciting, and glamorous. Consequently, some youth feel as though they are missing out on the fun of life because of the commandments. I have spoken with youth who have expressed jealousy toward those who joined the Church later in life because such people had the opportunity to "live it up" and "have some fun" before *having* to live the commandments.

Such attitudes toward the commandments result from not understanding the true purpose and motivation behind our Father in Heaven giving us commandments. The true doctrine is taught clearly in Mosiah 2:41. Let's look closely at a few lines from this verse.

"And moreover, I would desire that ye should consider on the blessed and happy state of those who keep the commandments of God."

Notice that King Benjamin described those who keep the commandments as "blessed" and "happy," not "restricted" or "boring" or "lame." To be "blessed" means to be made holy or to be protected or watched over. To be "happy" is to feel pleasure, joy, or contentment, or to feel satisfied that something is right or has been done right. Plug those definitions into the next part of the verse.

"And moreover, I would desire that ye should consider on the [protected, watched over, and pleasurable, joyful, content and satisfied] state of those who keep the commandments of God. For behold they are blessed [protected and watched over] in all things both temporal [earthly] and spiritual [eternal]."

An example here may help. I have associated with many young people who are wonderful but for whatever reason do not resist the urge to become involved in steady dating. Some rationalize their actions by convincing themselves that they are meant to be together or that they help each other be better. However, these justifications show a lack of understanding of the doctrine taught in Mosiah 2:41. As soon as we disregard the commandments and counsel of God, we put ourselves in danger of losing his help. Therefore that relationship may not be blessed or watched over like it would have been had the couple remained friends and avoided steady dating. If two youth in high school really, really like each other, they should do all they can to live in accordance with dating standards to make sure that the relationship remains "blessed."

As my wife and I were speaking to a large group of young women, my wife illustrated another way in which keeping the dating standards helps us to live in a "blessed and happy state." During the meeting we opened up some time for questions. One young lady came to the microphone and, through tears, asked the following: "How do you recover your self-esteem after you get dumped by a boy?" My wife's insightful answer showed an understanding of the doctrine taught in Mosiah 2:41. She responded, "It will be hard. You are not mature enough to handle the strong emotions associated with serious relationships yet. That is one of the reasons why a loving Heavenly Father has counseled young people your age not to be involved in steady dating. He was trying to save you from what you are feeling. If you will obey the commandments, you will be happier."

Is that true? Will you really be happier if you do not get involved in serious relationships in high school? Yes. Will you really be happier if you do not watch inappropriate media, do not listen to inappropriate music, do not dress and dance immodestly? Yes. Breaking such commandments may not seem like it brings regret, but it will. Remember, "wickedness never was happiness" (Alma 41:10).

If you keep the commandments, you will be blessed in all things: school, sports, choirs, friendships, fun—everything. This does not mean that life will be perfect and that you will make every team, get elected to every position, go to every dance, and get every good grade, but it does mean that God is watching over your life and that he will order things in such a way that they will be best for you. That is a very comforting state in which to live and helps one be "blessed and happy" even during the challenging teenage years.

Joseph Smith said that "Happiness is the object and design of our existence; and will be the end thereof, if we pursue the path that leads to it; and this path is . . . *keeping all the commandments of God.*"[1]

Elder Russell M. Nelson taught that "God . . . gave us commandments to live by, that we might have joy."[2]

Elder Joseph B. Wirthlin taught that "Some believe that the commandments of our Heavenly Father are restrictive and hard. To the contrary, they're a handbook to happiness. Every aspect of the gospel of Jesus Christ—the principles, the doctrines, and the commandments—is a part of our Heavenly Father's plan to help us obtain peace and happiness."[3]

When you understand the doctrine found in Mosiah 2:41, you'll appreciate the commandments for what they really are. The commandments are our God-given handbook to happiness. The commandments are not there simply to test us to see if we will do all things whatsoever the Lord our God shall command us. They are there to teach us how to be truly happy.

Imagine for a second that your grandmother made chocolate chip cookies that made your mouth water just thinking of them. You decided that you would ask her for the recipe so that you could enjoy them whenever you pleased. After obtaining the recipe, how closely would you follow it? Would you have any desire to add a cup of chopped up anchovies or perhaps some vinegar? I don't think so. Would you think your grandmother was being restrictive by giving you specific instructions instead of just letting you cook the way you wanted to? I hope not. I think you would follow the recipe as closely as possible so that you could bake and then eat some delicious cookies.

Commandments are much like a recipe that "cooks up" happiness and a fulfilling life.

My little brother Sheldon taught me something one time that has stuck with me ever since. He was speaking in reference to the parable of the prodigal son. In this parable a younger son went to his father and asked for his inheritance and then very soon after left his home and wasted his inherited property in "riotous living" and on harlots. A famine arose, and the young man found himself alone and hungry. He got a job taking care of a man's pig. At one point he became so hungry and destitute that he was looking upon the pigs with envy. He was so hungry even the pig slop looked good to him.

After some time, the boy "came to himself" and in a sense thought, "What in the world am I doing here? I am staring at pigs and envying their slop. My dad's servants are much better off than I am. I am going to go home and ask to be one of his servants." The boy had underestimated the love of his father. When he arrived home, his father welcomed him back and had a feast celebrating the return of his rebellious son.

Everyone was happy—that is, with the exception of his older brother. He refused to go to the feast. His father came out to him and asked him what the matter was. The son's reply, I feel, is very instructive:

Lo, these many years do I serve thee, neither transgressed I at any time thy commandment: and yet thou never gavest me a kid, that I might make merry with my friends:

But as soon as this thy son was come, which hath devoured thy living with harlots, thou hast killed for him the fatted calf. (Luke 15:29–30)

Sheldon taught me that it seems that the older brother feels as though the younger brother has gotten away with something here. It seems like the younger brother got to have his cake and eat it too. However, the older brother is forgetting or is not aware of a very important part of the story. He is forgetting the pigsty. The older brother never got so low in his life that he was staring at pigs and envying their slop. Among the many beautiful messages of forgiveness and repentance associated with this verse, Sheldon taught me another very important lesson: sin always leads to the pigsty. Wickedness never has nor will it ever lead to happiness.

From the beginning of time, Satan has tried to convince God's children that they are missing out on something by obeying God. When Adam and Eve were in the Garden of Eden, God told them they could freely eat of every tree in the garden with the exception of the tree of knowledge of good and evil. Adam and Eve definitely had more freedom in the Garden of Eden than they did restrictions. When Satan approached Eve in the garden, he asked her a question that revealed something about his character: "Ye shall not eat of every tree of the garden?" (Genesis 3:1). In other words "That's lame. God is not going to let you eat from all the trees?" His laser-beam focus was instantly directed toward the one tree Adam and Eve were told not to partake of.

Satan tries to do the same thing with us. There are so many virtuous, lovely, and praiseworthy things that we are not only allowed to partake of but are also commanded to seek after. There is so much wonderful music, art, television, and movies in the world that you could go your whole life and never run out of good stuff. It would take many lifetimes to participate in all of the many wholesome activities that are available to us. But Satan will try to get you to focus on all of the things that you can't partake of and will make them look as fun and as enticing as possible.

If you understand the doctrine of Mosiah 2:41, you will love the commandments, seek to learn them, and then strive as the sons of Helaman did to "obey . . . every word of command with exactness" (Alma 57:21) because you will know the commandments are the recipe for true and lasting happiness. You won't leave scripture study, prayer, seminary, church, temple attendance, family home evening, and mutual out of your life's recipe because you will know that you will be happier and more blessed by doing those things.

You will not add steady dating, pornography, inappropriate music and media, immorality, or violence to your recipe because you know that adding such "wickedness" can never lead to happiness (Alma 41:10). It is not in the recipe. The world will tell you that adding such ingredients will cook up a more delicious and exciting life; don't believe it. As so many have learned by sad experience, those ingredients will always leave a bitter aftertaste of guilt, shame, loss of confidence, and sadness. Speaking to a group of people who had added some of these ingredients to their lives, expecting it to cook up happiness, only to taste regret, Samuel the

Lamanite said, "ye have sought for happiness in doing iniquity, which thing is contrary to the nature of that righteousness which is in our great and Eternal Head" (Helaman 13:38).

So how can you apply Mosiah 2:41 to your life, and how can it help with high school? You can strive to talk the way God has told you to talk, read what God has told you to read, go where God has told you to go, date the way God tells you to date, and watch and listen to the kinds of things God wants you to. You can follow the recipe. Why? Because following God's recipe cooks up happiness—real, lasting happiness. If you are currently breaking a commandment, you are not as happy as you could be. If you will stop, repent, and live the commandments, your life will be happier. That is what Mosiah 2:41 teaches. That is the promise.

So the next time someone tries to make you feel as though you are missing out because of all those pesky commandments you have to live by, you can respond by saying:

It is written that we should "consider on the blessed and happy state of those that keep the commandments of God. For behold, they are blessed in all things, both temporal and spiritual; and if they hold out faithful to the end they are received into heaven, that thereby they may dwell with God in a state of never-ending happiness."

Notes

1. *Teachings of the Prophet Joseph Smith*, sel. Joseph Fielding Smith (Salt Lake City: Deseret Book, 1976), 255–56, emphasis added.
2. Russell M. Nelson, "'Joy Cometh in the Morning,'" *Ensign*, Nov. 1986, 67.
3. Joseph B. Wirthlin, "Three Choices," *Ensign*, Nov. 2003, 78.

3 james 1:14–15

TEMPTATION

To do something that you know is wrong to fit in with or to impress someone else.

IT IS WRITTEN

But every man is tempted, when he is drawn away of his own lust, and enticed. Then when lust hath conceived, it bringeth forth sin: and sin, when it is finished, bringeth forth death.

A COLLEAGUE of mine shared these verses in a meeting I was in as a young seminary teacher, and I have had a desire to share them with as many people as I could ever since. These verses are short, but they are packed with principles applicable to some degree to situations teenagers commonly face.

First let's deconstruct the scripture by turning it into a math equation. The equation may look something like this:

T = L + E

TEMPTATION = LUST + ENTICEMENT

In order to be tempted, two things must be present: lust and enticements. To lust means to have a strong desire to obtain something. A synonym for lust is "hunger for." *Enticement* is defined as something desirable that is offered. A couple of synonyms for *enticement* are *lure* or *bait*. So another way that this verse may read is: "Every man is tempted when he is drawn away by his own hunger and lured or baited."

With these definitions, the formula for temptation may be changed to:

T = H + L

TEMPTATION = HUNGER + LURE

This slight change sets up a fishing analogy that I think really helps us understand how the adversary works in our lives. First think about what a fisherman does when he is trying to catch a fish. He makes an artificial lure that looks like food to fish and sticks it on a hook. When the fish sees the lure, he thinks, "Mmmm . . . Food." He swims up and bites it, thinking it is going to fill his belly. But instead of filling his belly, the fish is now in pain. He is being pulled around by a force he had no idea even existed. He is yanked out of the water, and if the fisherman's objective is to find food, the fish is killed.

In this analogy, the fisherman is Satan, and you and I are the fish. You and I each have hungers. Those hungers are not necessarily bad. But Satan fashions lures to look like food that will fill our hungers. When we bite the lure, we realize that it does not fill our hunger. It brings only pain and regret.

Elder Ballard said, "Like the fly fisherman who knows that trout are driven by hunger, Lucifer knows our 'hunger,' or weaknesses, and tempts us with counterfeit lures which, if taken, can cause us to be yanked from the stream of life into his unmerciful influence. And unlike a fly fisherman who catches and releases the fish unharmed back into the water, Lucifer will not voluntarily let go. His goal is to make his victims as miserable as he is."[1]

Sharing the same analogy, Elder Marcus B. Nash of the Seventy said:

> Just as a fish in a mountain stream must be careful of the lures placed in its path to avoid being pulled away from the water, so must you and I be wise in order to avoid being pulled away from a happy, gospel-centered life. Remember that, as Lehi observed, the devil 'seeketh that all men might be miserable like unto himself' and obtains 'power to captivate' (2 Nephi 2:27, 29) us when we involve ourselves in unclean and evil things. Thus, do not be deceived into even nibbling at unworthy things, for Satan stands ready to set the hook. It was the very real risk of the hook being set subtly or suddenly that led the ancient prophet Moroni—who actually saw our day (see Mormon 8:35)—to pointedly warn you and me to 'touch not the evil gift, nor the unclean thing' (Moroni 10:30; emphasis added).[2]

Satan is a very scary character. Spencer W. Kimball said, "Lucifer and his followers know the habits, weaknesses, and vulnerable spots of everyone and take advantage of them to lead us to spiritual destruction."[3]

Joseph F. Smith said, "He [Satan] will lay temptations in the path of every individual to cause them to commit sin."[4] On another occasion President Smith wrote that "He [Satan] has power to place thoughts in our minds and to whisper to us in unspoken impressions to entice us to satisfy our appetites or desires and in various other ways he plays upon our weaknesses and desires."[5]

That is a very scary combination. Satan knows our weaknesses and vulnerable spots, has power to speak to us in unspoken impressions, and can place temptations in our path. Satan is not naïve to the hungers that teenagers experience. He stands at the ready to throw a lure that appears as though it will fill our hunger, and then he will try to get us to take the bait.

Remember it takes two things for us to be tempted, and we should recognize the difference between hungers and lures. They are not the same thing. One is not bad and could actually be God-given, and one is provided by Lucifer. One is given to help us reach our full potential in this life, and the other is given to bring us down and destroy us.

I would like to share two real-life examples that demonstrate how this might work. In my experience two hungers seem to drive a lot of what teenagers think, say, and do. They are the desire to be accepted by peers and the attraction to the opposite sex. Those hungers are not bad. As a matter of fact, I think that both are God-given hungers. But the following two accounts will illustrate how Satan may use them against us.

Hunger #1: The Desire to Be Accepted by Peers

God has created us in such a way that we need each other and want to be around people we love and who love us. President Gordon B. Hinckley counseled the youth in these words: "Everybody wants friends. Everybody needs friends. No one wishes to be without them. But never lose sight of the fact that it is your friends who will lead you along the paths that you will follow."[6]

Some of you may feel as though you walk each day in a sea of people you do not know well. You feel overwhelmed by the desire to have some friends to talk to, hang out with, and have fun with. At some point someone without strong moral standards may invite you to come over to his or her house. It may feel so refreshing to be invited, so you go. At some point the new friend may start laughing and say something like, "Do you drink?"

In this scenario, drinking alcohol is the lure. What you are hungering for is friendship and acceptance, but what gets thrown your way is alcohol. Like a lure to a fish, alcohol is not going to fill your hunger. It is a hook.

This is an example that is close to my heart. Someone that I love has struggled with drug addiction for a long time. He desperately wanted to stop and on one occasion asked if I would give him a priesthood blessing to help him in his efforts to stop. Before I gave him a blessing, we had a long talk. I asked him how he got caught up in drugs. He was a wonderful, vibrant, and intelligent young man who had let drugs suck so much of who he was out of his life. He told me that he was at a party one night with a young woman he wanted to impress. She handed him drugs, and he took them. He was not interested in drugs that night. He did not long for them. How could he? He had never had them. He had just been through some very tough experiences that had damaged his self-esteem, and he was afraid of letting down this young woman who was showing interest in him.

Can you see from this example how Satan works and why we should be so grateful for the commandments? Satan knew that this young man was hungering for this young lady's acceptance and attention, and Satan made him think that was what he was getting by taking drugs. What he received instead of this girl, who was soon out of his life, was an addiction that would change his life forever. I know that through the mercy and Atonement of the Savior, this young man can overcome his addiction, but even if he is able to do so, the price he will have paid to get off this hook will be great. He has already lost years of his life. The commandments will keep us out of dangerous waters and will help us identify lures.

Hunger #2: The Attraction to the Opposite Sex

It is obvious to me why God made us attracted to the opposite sex. If we are going to make it to the highest degree of the celestial kingdom, we will need to be married for time and for all eternity in the house of the Lord. This desire to be with the opposite sex really helps us keep that all-important commandment. You should never feel guilty for finding the opposite sex attractive even though sometimes temptations will come into your life because of those hungers. President Boyd K. Packer taught that "If you do not act on temptations, you need feel no guilt. They may be extremely difficult to resist. But that is better than to yield and bring disappointment and unhappiness to you and those who love you."[7]

I knew a young man once who was devastated after breaking the law of chastity. He had been dating a lot of different people, like he should have been, but there was one person who he became particularly attracted to. It was so much more exciting to go out with her than with anyone else. One night this young lady said to him, "We are both good kids and actually strengthen each other, don't you think? I think we will be okay if we don't date anyone else." He knew it would be wrong to do so but rationalized that it was okay as long as he did not break one of the "big commandments."

You may be able to see how one lure led to another in this young man's situation. He bit the lure of steady dating with the thought that dating other people was stupid because it was not as fun as dating each other, and the "we are both good kids and actually strengthen each other" argument was a rationalization. As these thoughts were entertained and the dating persisted, it led to a different kind of hunger. He hungered for the relationship to continue. As he became more and more familiar and comfortable with his girlfriend, on one occasion, she tried to take things way too far. This young man's attraction toward her, coupled with the fear of losing the relationship they had, made him susceptible to the dangerous lure of immorality, and he gave in to the temptation. Soon the relationship was over, and he was devastated for what he had done.

President Gordon B. Hinckley said the following to the youth of the Church, "And now just a word on the most common and most difficult of all problems for you young men and young women to handle. It is the relationship that you have one with another. You are dealing with the most powerful of human instincts. Only the will to live possibly exceeds it. The Lord has made us attractive one to another for a great purpose. But this very attraction becomes as a powder keg [barrel containing gunpowder] unless it is kept under control. It is beautiful when handled in the right way. It is deadly if it gets out of hand."[8]

Do you see how the commandments, even the "little ones," are designed to help us avoid these dangerous situations? Elder Nelson taught that "Because the evil one is ever at work, our vigilance cannot be relaxed—not even for a moment. A small and seemingly innocent invitation can turn into a tall temptation which can lead to tragic transgression. Night and day, at home or away, we must shun sin and 'hold fast that which is good.'"[9]

These two scenarios are just examples to illustrate how Satan uses lures to tempt and trap men. There are many other hungers and countless other lures. So how do you distinguish a lure from real food? As we listen to the counsel of prophets and apostles, Satan's lures become pretty easy to detect. Alma warned that "wickedness never was happiness" (Alma 41:10). Another way to say that phrase is that wickedness will never truly fill your hungers. I love what Moroni teaches on this subject:

> But behold, that which is of God inviteth and enticeth to do good continually; wherefore, every thing which inviteth and enticeth to do good, and to love God, and to serve him, is inspired of God.
>
> Wherefore, take heed, my beloved brethren, that ye do not judge that which is evil to be of God, or that which is good and of God to be of the devil. (Moroni 7:13–14)

The commandments and the spirit of the Lord will let you know "with a perfect knowledge" what is right and what is wrong. Another way to say that is the commandments and the spirit of the Lord will let you know what is a lure and what is real food.

The gospel of Jesus Christ offers us real food. President Ezra Taft Benson said, "Men and women who turn their lives over to God will discover that He can make a lot more out of their lives than they can. He will deepen their joys, expand their vision, quicken their minds, strengthen their muscles, lift their spirits, multiply their blessings, increase their opportunities, comfort their souls, raise up friends, and pour out peace."[10] God offers us real food. Satan offers us lures.

I hope the next time that Satan tries to offer you a lure, you will recognize that it will never fill your hunger. I also hope that you will be able to respond by thinking to yourself, "I know I have hungers, but what you are offering is not food; it is a lure, and it will not fill my hunger but will actually hurt me. It is written that "every man is tempted, when he is drawn away of his own lust [hunger], and enticed [lured]. Then when lust hath conceived, it bringeth forth sin: and sin, when it is finished, bringeth forth death" (James 1:14–15). Think to yourself, "I don't want to die spiritually, so I am not going to bite your lure."

Notes

1. M. Russell Ballard, "O That Cunning Plan of the Evil One," *Ensign*, Nov. 2010, 108–10.
2. Marcus B. Nash, "The Great Plan of Happiness," *Ensign*, Nov. 2006, 49–50.
3. Spencer W. Kimball, *The Miracle of Forgiveness* (Salt Lake City: Bookcraft, 1969), 218–19.
4. Joseph Fielding Smith, *Answers to Gospel Questions* (Salt Lake City: Deseret Book, 1960), 3:81.
5. Ibid.
6. Gordon B. Hinckley, "A Prophet's Counsel and Prayer for Youth," *Ensign*, Jan. 2001, 2.

7. Boyd K. Packer, "Ye Are the Temple of God," *Ensign*, Nov. 2000, 72–74.

8. Gordon B. Hinckley, "A Prophet's Counsel and Prayer for Youth," *Ensign*, Jan. 2001, 2.

9. Russell M. Nelson, "Set in Order Thy House," *Ensign*, Nov. 2001, 71.

10. Ezra Taft Benson, *The Teachings of Ezra Taft Benson* (Salt Lake City: Bookcraft, 1998), 361.

4 2 nephi 32:8-9

TEMPTATION

To not say your prayers, either out of laziness or because you feel guilty for something you have done.

IT IS WRITTEN

And now, my beloved brethren, I perceive that ye ponder still in your hearts; and it grieveth me that I must speak concerning this thing. For if ye would hearken unto the Spirit which teacheth a man to pray ye would know that ye must pray; for the evil spirit teacheth not a man to pray, but teacheth him that he must not pray.

But behold, I say unto you that ye must pray always, and not faint; that ye must not perform any thing unto the Lord save in the first place ye shall pray unto the Father in the name of Christ, that he will consecrate thy performance unto thee, that thy performance may be for the welfare of thy soul.

HIGH school is a very important time. You have so many decisions to make, things to do, and relationships to maintain or develop. It is also a very tough time.

I remember my high school days being some of the best and worst times of my life. It seems that the highs are often followed by the lows. The Lord has given us the wonderful blessing of prayer to help us through high school.

You may be familiar with this phrase that is sometimes printed on the outside of boxes: "Fragile: Handle with Care." I walked into a house one time and saw a play on that phrase written on the wall in vinyl lettering. The wall read, "Life is fragile; handle with prayer." That phrase impressed me because at the time I felt pretty fragile. I think some of you could relate to the word *fragile*. To be fragile means to be easily broken or unlikely to withstand severe stresses or strains. Have you ever felt so stressed about school or friends or sports or whatever that you feel like you could barely stand it? Have you felt like your heart is broken easily or often by friends or situations like not making the team or not getting the part or not getting asked to the dance? If your answer is yes, then I would pass on to you a modified version of the play on words above: "High school is a fragile time; handle with prayer."

If I could go back and talk to my high school self, I would definitely share the above scripture with myself. This scripture teaches some very important doctrines about prayer. I would like to point out a couple of things that these wonderful verses teach us about prayer.

1. "The evil spirit teacheth not a man to pray, but teacheth him that he must not pray."

This is a very important line. If you ever feel like you should not pray, that feeling is not coming from Heavenly Father; it is coming from the evil spirit. At times in my life, I have done things that I should not have done. In those times I have been tempted to avoid God and not pray to him. Some may mistake that feeling of guilt to mean that God does not want to talk to them. I am sure the adversary loves when we feel this way. When we make a mistake, we need to go to God to be made whole. To stay away from him in such situations is like having a toothache but not going to the dentist because you feel guilty for not flossing. Just as the dentist is the one who can heal you and take away the pain and discomfort you are feeling, the Savior is the only one who can take away the pain and discomfort of guilt.

When Adam and Eve were in the Garden of Eden and had just partaken of the forbidden fruit, they heard the voice of the Lord and "went to hide themselves from the presence of the Lord" (Moses 4:14). I am certain that this feeling to hide from God was prompted by Satan. God asked Adam and Eve a question that I think he would ask each of us if we ever tried to hide from him because we were ashamed of something we had done: "Where goest thou?" (Moses 4:15). Another way to say that may be, "Where are you going? Are you going to run and hide, or are you going to come unto me and get help?" Satan wanted them to stay away from the one being who could help them overcome the Fall. Likewise, when we fall, Satan also wants us to run and hide. Don't do it. Get on your knees and pray to God for help. Who cares if you don't feel like praying, and who cares why you don't feel like doing so—it does not matter if you are feeling guilty, angry or frustrated with God, or just brokenhearted; get down on your knees and pray. President Brigham Young taught, "It matters not whether you or I feel like praying, when the time comes to pray, pray. If we do not feel like it, we should pray till we do."[1]

I know what it feels like to have the adversary make me feel unworthy to pray to God. I also know what it feels like to wonder why God would let something horrible happen to me or my family to the point that I am so frustrated I am not in the mood to pray. I also know of the comfort and help that comes into our life when we talk to God about those frustrations. Remember, God will never prompt you not to pray; only Satan will. That is a very important doctrine that this verse teaches.

2. "Ye must pray always."

This is a simple line, but there are a couple of really important applications in those four words. It is important to be consistent in our prayers. High school is a busy time of life, but if you ever get too busy to pray, then you are too busy.

We have been given the following scriptural counsel: "Counsel with the Lord in all thy doings, and he will direct thee for good; yea, when thou liest down at night lie down unto the Lord, that he may watch over you in your sleep; and when thou risest in the morning let thy heart be full of thanks unto God; and if ye do these things, ye shall be lifted up at the last day" (Alma 37:37).

Sometimes we are lazy with our prayers. Have you ever lain down in your nice, comfortable bed and then realized that you did not say your prayers? Instead of getting out of bed and kneeling next to it, I have sometimes lazily turned myself into a giant roly-poly and attempted to pray under my warm covers. I have to laugh at myself when I think of this. After all, how hard is it to roll over and let gravity take over? When I make an effort to put myself in a position to really think about what I want to say, my prayers are more sincere. When I lie in bed and "get my prayer over with," I think I miss out on some blessings.

I know that one of the major challenges for teenagers is morning prayers. Mornings are often rushed. I have spoken to many teenagers who say their morning prayers while walking out the door with breakfast in hand, backpack on, and a worried, hurried mind. I know that taking a couple of minutes to kneel in humble prayer and talk to God about the day's activities will be of far greater value than that extra five minutes of sleep you received from hitting the snooze button. After all, when was the last time you hit snooze on the alarm and actually woke up a lot more refreshed the next time the alarm sounded? Making time for prayer in the morning will be much more of a blessing to your day than hitting the snooze button.

You and I have been counseled to pray when "ye are in your fields. . . . Cry unto him in your houses. . . . Pour out your souls in your closets, and your secret places, and in your wilderness" (Alma 34: 20–21, 26). We might change this to fit our circumstances to read, "Cry to him in your classrooms; on the football, baseball, or soccer field; or on the wrestling mat. Cry to him in the dance or choir room. Cry to him in your bedroom, on your hikes, and during your hunts."

Life is bound to be busy, but remember, you don't need to kneel all the time to pray. The fact that God has commanded you to pray always suggests that he does not expect you to kneel each time you pray. Though it is good to kneel and show respect when appropriate, you can't spend your whole life on your knees. Elder Russell M. Nelson of the Quorum of the Twelve Apostles taught that "We often kneel to pray; we may stand or be seated. Physical position is less important than is spiritual submission to God."[2] Just talk to him. In other words, "ye must pray always." You will be blessed if you do.

3. "Ye must not perform anything unto the Lord save in the first place ye shall pray."

I sometimes do an activity with youth where I break them up into groups and have them make a list of the top five things that weigh upon the minds of the youth of the Church. A few topics come up almost every time: school, relationships with friends, the future (college, mission, marriage, and so on), extracurricular activities (sports, choir, band, and so on), and family.

After doing this activity, I joke with them that if I were to judge their worries based upon the prayers I heard them say in my class, I would think that driving home safely was their number one concern. That is odd to me because I have witnessed the way they drive. I have a hard time believing that the most pressing issue on a teenager's mind at seven in the morning is "getting home safely when the time comes." I know that praying in front of a class is not the time to get personal, but I do think that sometimes we can fall into the trap of vain repetition that the Savior has warned about. If something is vain, it means it is devoid of substance or meaning. Have you ever said a prayer just to say a prayer, without concentrating on what you were saying? Have you got into a pattern of saying the same thing all the time without really talking to God from your heart? I think it is important to talk to God about those things that you are really concerned about. Talk with him about that frustrating teacher or assignment. Talk with God about that friend who seems to be giving you the cold shoulder. Talk with God about that temptation that seems to be constantly pressing upon you. Talk to him about the game or the performance coming up. Talk to him about your hopes, dreams, doubts, and fears. He is your Father, and he wants to talk to you about things that really matter to you.

I remember receiving a challenge one time that really blessed my life. I was told to sit on my bed and think for one minute about what I really wanted to talk to God about before I got down on my knees and prayed. This practice has been a great blessing to me and has helped me make my prayers more meaningful. One youth told me that her prayers have been enhanced by writing in her journal each night before she prays. I encourage you to make an effort to make your prayers more meaningful if you feel as if they could use a boost.

The Bible Dictionary says under the topic of prayer that "the object of prayer is not to change the will of God, but to secure for ourselves and for others blessings that God is already willing to grant, but that are made conditional on our asking for them." In other words, there are some blessings you could have but will not receive without asking for them. As you talk with God about the things that matter most to you, you will be blessed in those areas of your life in ways that you would not be blessed if you did not talk with God about them. "Ye must not perform anything unto the Lord save in the first place ye shall pray." God cares about all that's going on in your life.

I have been taught much about prayer from my children. When my oldest child, Emma, was about four years old, we had an experience as a family that really strengthened her faith in prayer. We had just returned home to Utah from a weekend trip to my parents' house in Idaho, and my wife could not find her purse. We thought we had left it at a gas station on the way home. We were worried because all of our bank cards were in her purse. We looked everywhere we could think to look. Before we called and cancelled our cards, we knelt as a family to pray. In the middle of the prayer I received an impression to look in my wife's dance bag. I stood up and went to the closet, where I found her purse. It turns out that we had never taken it with us on our trip.

This had a big effect upon Emma. She became convinced that if she prayed about something, Heavenly Father would tell her dad the answer. Soon after this experience, she lost her stuffed bunny that she slept with each night. It is special to her because her Great-Grandpa Hope gave it to her. She said, "Dad, let's pray and ask Heavenly Father where it is." We knelt to pray, and she said the prayer: "Dear Heavenly Father, I have lost my bunny that Great-Grandpa Hope gave me. Will you tell my daddy where it is? Thank you. In the name of Jesus Christ, amen." She sat up, looked at me, and said, "Well, where is it?" I was about to give her a speech about how prayer really works, when I had the simple thought to look in her closet. There it was, in her laundry basket under some dirty clothes.

A short time later, she lost an outline I had helped her prepare for our family home evening. Once again, she prayed, "Dear Heavenly Father, I have lost my family home evening lesson. Will you tell my daddy where it is? Thank you. In the name of Jesus Christ, amen." Once again she looked at me and said, "Where is it?" Once again I began to think of how I could break it to her how prayer really works. As I was gathering my thoughts, I had the impression to go check in the pants of the suit I was wearing the day before when I helped her prepare the lesson. There it was.

A short time later my girls lost the MP3 players they had just received for their birthdays. We looked everywhere for them and could not find them. My girls were heartbroken. Once again Emma prayed, "Dear Heavenly Father, I have lost my iPod (that is what she called it). I don't care if it is tonight or tomorrow or the next day, but it is really special to me. Will you tell my daddy where it is? Thank you. In the name of Jesus Christ, amen." She sat up, looked at me, and once again asked, "Well, where is it?" I thought this was the time when I would have to teach her about prayer and how it really works. I had a speech prepared about being responsible with our things and how if we are not responsible we can't rely on God to do for us what we did not do for ourselves, but fearing that I would damage the sweet and simple testimony Emma had in prayer, I told her we would wake up in the morning and look for them when it was light.

We went to bed, and when I woke up in the dark of the morning, I told my wife to look in the backyard when it got light again because I had a thought that they might be out there. She went in the backyard later and found the MP3 players sitting in a puddle of water. My two-year-old had hauled them out there and left them, and it had rained all night.

I was relieved that we found them. I came home from work about the same time my daughter got home from school. I walked in to find her kneeling at our bed next to my wife. She prayed and asked if her iPod could still work even though it got wet and thanked Heavenly Father for helping her to find it. The MP3 players work to this day.

The whole time I was thinking that eventually I was going to have to teach my daughter how prayer "actually works." I did not realize that she and Heavenly Father were teaching me about prayer.

A little while after these experiences, my wife and I were having automobile problems. If anyone reading this book would like advice on how to buy a bad car for a bad price, I would be happy to let you in on my secrets. I have not had good luck with buying cars. Anyway, I had just got the dealership to agree to fix something on the car I had just purchased that was supposed to be fixed when we got it. They kindly gave me a rental car to drive. It was a very nice truck with a Hemi engine. Oh, how I loved that truck for the week I drove it. The last night I had the truck, I was on my way to a BYU football game, and my wife was following me to have a hamburger with me before the game. She called me and asked if I knew about the dent in the bumper of the truck. I had never seen it, but I was sure I did not do it.

I began to get really frustrated and worried. We did not have the money to pay for our insurance to fix a very expensive bumper. I was sitting at the table in the restaurant, visibly shaken. My wife told me it would all work out, but I was frustrated. "How could we be so unlucky?" I asked her. "The harder we try, the worse it gets." She told me to go have fun at the game. As I got up to leave, I said a prayer in my heart to Heavenly Father. I asked him to please help it work out. I knew

I had not caused that dent in the bumper and asked for his help in not being held responsible for it. I was taking my second daughter Ella to the game with me. We walked out of the mall, and she began to jump up and down singing the Cougar Fight song.

A man in the parking lot approached us to tell me how cute Ella was. He said, "I can't find my girlfriend's car." He had been wandering around the parking lot looking for it. I asked if there was anything I could do to help. He said that he just had to walk around until he found it. As we approached the rental truck and as I said good-bye to him, he pointed to the truck and said, "Is this a rental?" I told him that it was. He then told me that he had rented that truck last weekend. I asked him if the dent was in the bumper, and he said that it was. I got his name and number just in case it was not in the paperwork of my rental agreement.

I drove away in wonder. Of the tens of thousands of people in Utah Valley, this gentleman was wandering around the parking lot at the very time I was coming out. I said a prayer of gratitude and repented for being so slow to turn to God for help.

I testify that God answers our prayers. He will not always answer our prayers as immediately as the examples above illustrate; I only share them to demonstrate the point that even when we are not answered in the way we would like or as quickly as we would like, we can take comfort in the fact that he does hear us. The scripture 2 Nephi 32:8–9 teaches us to "pray always" and "not perform anything unto the Lord save in the first place ye shall pray . . . in the name of Christ, that he will consecrate thy performance unto thee, that thy performance may be for the welfare of thy soul."

Nephi knew what a blessing it was to pray unto the Lord. He also knew the negative effects of not praying. I think his willingness to get down on his knees is what set him apart from his brothers, Laman and Lemuel. They went through virtually the same experience with completely different outcomes. When their father told them they were to leave Jerusalem and go into the desert, Laman and Lemuel murmured and complained against their father. Nephi cried unto the Lord, and the Lord visited him and softened his heart so that he would believe all the words that had been spoken by his father (1 Nephi 2:16).

When their father had the vision of the tree of life, Laman and Lemuel sat around and complained about how confused they were (1 Nephi 15:1–10). Nephi, on the other hand, prayed that he might see and hear and know of the things that his father saw (1 Nephi 10:17–19). He was given a guided tour of his father's dream by an angel.

When Nephi broke his bow, his brothers were angry and murmured exceedingly. Nephi made a bow out of wood, went to his father, and asked him to pray and ask the Lord where he might go to obtain food. He was led to a place where he obtained food for their family (1 Nephi 16:16–32).

When Nephi was commanded to build a ship, his brothers murmured, mocked, and refused to help. Nephi prayed unto the Lord to find out where he might go to find ore to make tools. The Lord not only directed him to the ore to make tools but also gave him instructions how to build the ship that sailed his family safely to the promised land (1 Nephi 17).

To me it is significant that Nephi chooses as some of his last words to us this scripture:

> And now, my beloved brethren, I perceive that ye ponder still in your hearts; and it grieveth me that I must speak concerning this thing. For if ye would hearken unto the Spirit which teacheth a man to pray, ye would know that ye must pray; for the evil spirit teacheth not a man to pray, but teacheth him that he must not pray.
>
> But behold, I say unto you that ye must pray always, and not faint; that ye must not perform any thing unto the Lord save in the first place ye shall pray unto the Father in the name of Christ, that he will consecrate thy performance unto thee, that thy performance may be for the welfare of thy soul.

I think his ability to do what he asked us to do was one of the things that made Nephi great. I think it will make us great if we turn to the Lord more as well.

I hope that when the adversary tries to convince us in any way either not to pray or to take prayer lightly, we will respond with, "It is written that 'the evil spirit teacheth not a man to pray.' I need to pray always and not perform anything unto the Lord save in the first place I pray." I know as we do so we will be blessed for it.

Notes

1. John A. Widtsoe, ed., *Discourses of Brigham Young* (Salt Lake City: Bookcraft, 1988), 44.
2. Russell M. Nelson, "Sweet Power of Prayer," *Ensign*, May 2003, 7.

5 alma 29:1-3

TEMPTATION

To not like yourself and wish you were somebody else.

IT IS WRITTEN

O that I were an angel, and could have the wish of mine heart, that I might go forth and speak with the trump of God, with a voice to shake the earth, and cry repentance unto every people!

Yea, I would declare unto every soul, as with the voice of thunder, repentance and the plan of redemption, that they should repent and come unto our God, that there might not be more sorrow upon all the face of the earth.

But behold, I am a man, and do sin in my wish; for I ought to be content with the things which the Lord hath allotted unto me.

HAVE you ever wished you were someone or something other than yourself? If so, you are in pretty good company. Elder Jeffrey R. Holland of the Quorum of the Twelve Apostles said, "Almost everyone at some time or other wants to be something they are not!"[1] One of those people who wished they were something they were not was Alma the Younger. He is often praised for his desire to be an angel instead of a prophet so that he could cry repentance to every people, but Alma called this a sin. After saying "O that I were an angel," Alma said, "[But I] do sin in my wish; for I ought to be content with the things which the Lord hath allotted unto [or prearranged for] me."

You may not walk around school wishing you were an angel, but I know it is common for teenagers to walk around wishing they were something they are not. I did a survey of a group of young people once and asked them if they had ever wished they were someone else, and if yes, when. Almost every one of them responded that they had. Here are some of their reasons for doing so:

"When I went prom dress shopping, it was so frustrating because none of the dresses were fitting the way I wanted. . . . I wished I was someone else, someone skinnier, taller, and more beautiful."

"There are days when I am told I am fat or ugly and I go outside and sit in the grass and wish that something magical will happen and I won't look like what other people say is unsightly or uncomfortable."

"I was cut from the basketball team. When I saw the guys on the team hanging out at lunch or warming up for the game or being cheered in the pep rally, I wished I could have been any of those guys on the team."

"I worked so hard, and I still did not get accepted to the college I wanted to go to. My friend got a scholarship. I wish I was him!"

"My dad lost his job and our family had no money. I watched all of the other kids with their cars and clothes and phones that I could not afford. I must admit there were a few times I wished I could be someone who had those things."

"I feel all of the time like I'm not important. I'm just that person over there. I wish I had better social skills like everyone else does. I want to be someone important."

Can you relate with any of these concerns? I know I can. I remember a time in my life when my face broke out really bad. I remember looking at my friends with perfectly clear complexions, wishing that I had their skin. It was a tough time for me, and it was hard to appreciate the body that I had been given. Like Alma, I found myself wishing, "O that I . . ." Do you see how we could take my concerns and your concerns, whatever they are, and plug them into the verse above, and it would read much the same?

O that I were skinnier . . .

O that I were prettier . . .

O that I were more athletic . . .

O that I were smarter . . .

O that I were richer . . .

O that I were more popular and social . . .

In each case I think that the verse could end the same way as it did for Alma. "[But] I do sin in my wish, for I ought to be content with the things that the Lord hath allotted unto me."

Being content with the things that the Lord has allotted is a lot easier said than done, but there are some doctrines that, if we understood them in our hearts, would help us become more content with ourselves. Let's explore a few of those.

The first idea that might help comes from Elder Neal A. Maxwell. He taught that "the same God that placed that star in a precise orbit millennia before it appeared over Bethlehem in celebration of the birth of the Babe has given at least equal attention to placement of each of us in precise human orbits."[2]

What does that mean? I think he is saying that it is no accident that we are who we are, that we have the talents we have, that we look the way we look and were born into the family we were born into. Each of those things places us in a "human orbit" that will allow us to have the experiences and come in contact with the people that are necessary for us to reach our full potential. Just as the star was placed in orbit to appear over Bethlehem, you have been placed in human orbits so that at certain times in your life you will be in just the right moment to use your abilities and talents to bless and help others. If you looked different or had different talents, you may not be where you are supposed to be to do what you are supposed to do and to meet who you are supposed to meet. Knowing this helps me be content with myself. I don't need to be great in every way I wish I were great; I just need to be me. That is what Heavenly Father wants me to be. I need to be the best me I can be, and when who I am conflicts with gospel principles, I should repent and change. God will help us with that. But I should never obsess over trying to be something I was not created to be. I should use my talents and abilities and energies to do whatever I can in my orbit to bless, lead, and comfort others. That is what I have control over, and it is a lot better to worry about things I can control than obsess over things I cannot.

The second doctrine that we need to understand that will help us to be more content with ourselves is that you are a literal child of God. You are probably familiar with the story of the ugly duckling. In this story, a mother duck notices that one of her new chicks is a lot bigger and looks different than the other chicks. The ugly duckling grows up being picked on and teased by the other ducks. One day as he separates himself from the teasing, he sees a flock of absolutely beautiful white birds flying overhead. At the same time the "ugly duckling" looks into the water and sees his reflection. He realizes that he looks just like those beautiful birds. He realizes that he is a beautiful swan and not an ugly duckling.

Some of you who read this book may feel picked at and teased for your appearance or uniqueness. Please know that you are not an ugly duckling and you are even more than a swan. You are a son or daughter of God. Your destiny is to become like him. Speaking of this story, President Dieter F. Uchtdorf said, "Like this young swan, most of us have felt at one time or another that we don't quite fit in. Much of the confusion we experience in this life comes from simply not understanding who we are. Too many go about their lives thinking they are of little worth when, in reality, they are elegant and eternal creatures of infinite value with potential beyond imagination."[3]

My daughter's elementary school was putting on the play *101 Dalmatians*, and she wanted to participate. She worked hard practicing the song for her audition at home, and the day arrived for her to perform. I went and watched as she nervously stood in front of a third-grade teacher and sang her song with all of her heart. On the day they gave everyone their parts, I picked up Emma from her school. I watched as she kindly hugged all of her friends good-bye and then jumped into the back of my car. I asked her how her practice was. As I watched her in my mirror, I saw huge alligator tears form in her eyes and then tumble down her cheeks. I asked her what was wrong. She responded, "I got a non-speaking puppy part." We talked about how every part in the play was important, and she went on to do her part very well. She had a marvelous time doing so and made her parents proud.

Some of you may feel as though you have been given a "nonspeaking puppy part" in life. I assure you there is no such thing. In Doctrine and Covenants section 78, the Lord encourages the members of his church to "come up unto the crown prepared for you, and be made rulers over many kingdoms" (v. 15). Who receives crowns? Royalty receives crowns. If you know you are a child of God, you will realize that you are literally royalty, a prince or a princess and a king and a queen in waiting. This should help us be content with who we are.

The third doctrine comes from President Ezra Taft Benson. He said, "If we love God, do His will, and fear His judgment more than men's, we will have self-esteem."[4] That is a short statement, but I think that it teaches a really important principle. If we worry more about what God thinks of us than man, we will feel better about ourselves.

When I was a teenager struggling with some of these issues, this statement really helped me. My life's experience has taught me that people are not always nice. Sometimes people are not only hoping that you look bad but also trying to make you look bad. They can take a good thing that you do or wonderful accomplishments you achieve and out of jealousy or envy turn those good things against you. You will go crazy trying to please everyone. It is impossible. But you don't need to please everyone. You need to concentrate on pleasing God. You need to do your best to keep his commandments and repent when you make a mistake. God does not judge you or attribute value to you based upon your looks or whether you make the team or your test score. One way to overcome the desire to be someone else is to seek vertical praise instead of horizontal praise. In other words, like the swan in the story of the ugly duckling, we need to look up to realize who we are and what our worth is. What God thinks of us should be our number one concern, and as it becomes such, President Benson says, we will have self-esteem. Don't listen to the quacking ducks on the TV or the quacking ducks at school who are simply trying to make themselves feel better by making others feel worse. Look up to God to know what you are really worth.

To be clear, the message of this chapter is definitely not "don't shower, don't exercise, and don't take care of your body. Don't work hard in school or practice diligently in your extracurricular activities. Be content with exactly who you are and don't try to improve yourself." That attitude of laziness and complacency is not acceptable to the Lord. The message is simply this: When the adversary tries to convince you that you are of little or no worth, I hope you will be able to respond, "It is written that 'I ought to be content with the things which the Lord hath allotted unto me' because I am a child of God with infinite potential to become like him." I also pray that instead of going throughout your high school years saying "O that I were . . . more beautiful or handsome or athletic or smart or . . ." you will be able to say,

"O that I were . . . me. I am happy being me because I know that being me will help me become all that I can become."

Notes

1. Jeffrey R. Holland, "To Young Women," *Ensign*, Nov. 2005, 28.
2. Neal A. Maxwell, *That My Family Should Partake* (Salt Lake City: Deseret Book, 1974), 86.
3. Dieter F. Uchtdorf, "The Reflection in the Water," CES Fireside for Young Adults, Nov. 1, 2009, Brigham Young University.
4. Ezra Taft Benson, "Beware of Pride," *Ensign*, May 1989, 4.

6 2 corinthians 4:17-18

TEMPTATION

To feel that God must not care about you because of the trials you are experiencing.

IT IS WRITTEN

For our light affliction, which is but for a moment, worketh for us a far more exceeding and eternal weight of glory;

While we look not at the things which are seen, but at the things which are not seen: for the things which are seen are temporal; but the things which are not seen are eternal.

A LOT of things can go wrong in high school. Friends turn on you, coaches cut you from the team, you miss the shot or drop the pass, you don't get the part, or you are not asked to the dance. Sometimes tests are failed, rumors are started, the other person is voted in, or—and maybe this is the toughest—you feel as though if you were to disappear no one would even notice.

When faced with such trials, you may be tempted to ask yourself why a loving Father in Heaven would allow you to go through such a hard time. The answer may lie in remembering that God is not just interested in keeping us happy; he is trying to help us become something. The scripture 2 Corinthians 4:17–18 teaches that Heavenly Father is willing to let us experience "light affliction" if it will "work for us a far more exceeding and eternal weight of glory." Two things are compared in this verse: weight and time.

First pay attention to the reference of weight in this scripture. It is comparing the weight of our affliction to the weight of the glory that comes from it. Our "light affliction" is nothing compared to the "exceeding [enormous] weight of glory" that comes from the affliction. Now look at the time comparison. Our light afflictions, which are "but for a moment," work for us a far more exceeding and "eternal" weight of glory. In other words, trials and affliction don't last forever, but what we become because of them does.

Elder Dallin H. Oaks taught that "the gospel of Jesus Christ challenges us to *become* something. . . . Our needed conversions are often achieved more readily by suffering and adversity than by comfort and tranquility. . . . Most of us experience some measure of what the scriptures call 'the furnace of affliction' (Isa. 48:10; 1 Ne. 20:10). . . . Through the justice and mercy of a loving Father in Heaven, the refinement and sanctification possible through such experiences can help us achieve what God desires us to become."[1]

President Spencer W. Kimball wrote that "No pain that we suffer, no trial that we experience is wasted. It ministers to our education . . . , to the development of such qualities as patience, faith, fortitude [strength and endurance in a difficult or painful situation] and humility. All that we suffer and all that we endure, especially when we endure it patiently, builds up our characters, purifies our hearts, expands our souls, and makes us more tender and charitable, more worthy to be called the children of God . . . and it is through sorrow and suffering, toil and tribulation, that we gain the education that we come here to acquire and which will make us more like our Father and Mother in heaven."[2]

It is evident from these teachings that God will let you go through tough times to help you become what you need to become. Afflictions, rejections, difficulties, burdens, problems, hardships, pain, trouble, misery, and misfortune all mold us into what God knows we can become. You may have had a coach, instructor, or teacher who has put you through a lot of discomfort. You may have even resented that person for doing so as you were running or rehearsing more than you desired or even more than you thought you could. But then there may have come a moment when you realized that they had helped you become a better athlete, singer, musician, or student. At that time, hopefully you appreciated them for helping you improve. In my experience the most beloved coaches and teachers are not those who let the people under their care do whatever makes them comfortable; rather it is those who see the potential in the people they lead and do all they can to help them reach that potential.

Our Heavenly Father sees past what we are to what we can become and is willing to allow us to experience "light afflictions" that last "but for a moment" if they will bring about a far more "[enormous] and eternal weight of glory." Look at verse 18 and pay attention to the way we are encouraged to look at things:

"While we look not at the things which are seen, but at the things which are not seen: for the things which are seen are temporal; but the things which are not seen are eternal."

Another way of saying this might be that we need to have an eternal perspective and fix our eyes not on what is seen but on what is not seen, because what is seen (the trial), is temporary but what is not seen (what God is helping us become because of the trial) is eternal.

James E. Faust, former member of the first presidency, said that one of the reasons we go through tough times even when we are trying so hard to be good is that God "loves *us* so much more than he loves our happiness."[3] What does that mean? An experience I had with my oldest daughter helped me understand better my relationship with my Heavenly Father, especially as it pertains to the suffering he allows me to experience in this life.

My wife was expecting our second child, and we went in as a family for my wife's checkup. While we were at the doctor's office, they realized that my oldest daughter was past due for some shots. She was almost two years old and had just started to talk. I went with her and some nurses into another room while my wife finished her checkup. When we got into the room, I laid her down on the hospital bed and held her down, looking into her face and smiling. She looked up at me and smiled with a bewildered look on her face that seemed to ask, "What are you doing, Dad?" The nurses exposed her little thighs and rubbed on some alcohol, which she seemed to find amusing. Then they gave her a couple of shots in each leg. Her smile quickly melted into sobs. The nurses put bandages on her legs and let her stand up. She gave me a hug and cried for a minute, then backed up, grabbed both of my cheeks, looked straight into my eyes, and through her tears yelled, "NO, NO, Daddy! Naughty!"

I realized at that moment that all I could do was tell her that I loved her and hold her tight. In her little mind, her daddy had just held her down and let others stick her with needles. Imagine her twenty-two-month-old face if I would have sat her down and said, "Sweetie, Daddy is not naughty. We just injected you with a serum that contained a killed or weakened part of a germ that is responsible for an infection that if you caught would result in things much worse than a shot. Because the germ has been killed or weakened it will not make you sick, but rather your body will react by making protective substances called antibodies. Your antibodies are your body's defenders because they help to kill off the germs that enter your body. In other words, the shots you just received exposed you safely to germs so that you can become protected from a disease without having to come down with the disease."

Such an explanation might have been more painful to her than the shot. I knew that the shots would hurt my daughter, but I also believed that if my daughter knew what I knew she would rather have a little shot than a life-altering or life-ending disease. In other words her light affliction, which would last but for a moment, would work for her a far more enormous blessing when compared to the disease that could follow if she were not to get the shot. This taught me a lot about my relationship with my Heavenly Father. We are little babies in comparison to his great knowledge. The Lord told the Saints in the Doctrine and Covenants:

> Verily, verily, I say unto you, ye are little children, and ye have not as yet understood how great blessings the Father hath in his own hands and prepared for you;
>
> And ye cannot bear all things now; nevertheless, be of good cheer, for I will lead you along. The kingdom is yours and the blessings thereof are yours, and the riches of eternity are yours. (D&C 78:17–18)

On another occasion he taught them:

> Ye cannot behold with your natural eyes, for the present time, the design of your God concerning those things which shall come hereafter, and the glory which shall follow after much tribulation.
>
> For after much tribulation come the blessings. Wherefore the day cometh that ye shall be crowned with much glory; the hour is not yet, but is nigh at hand. (D&C 58:3–4)

Just as my daughter could not see or understand why I would hold her down and let ladies stick her with sharp needles, you may not understand why God allows you to go through the afflictions you will experience. However, time has a way of helping you understand.

President Uchtdorf shared a story in general conference that illustrated this principle. He grew up in Germany, and when he was eleven years old, his family was forced to leave East Germany and begin a new life in West Germany. His parents began to operate a laundry business in town, and he was the delivery boy. He had a heavy black bicycle that he rode around with the heavy laundry cart on the back. He was not excited to do so. At times he felt as though his lungs were going to burst from the strain of pulling the cart.

Later in life he decided to become an air force pilot. In the process of becoming a pilot he had to have an extensive physical. At the conclusion of the physical, the doctors announced, "You have scars on your lung which are an indication of a lung disease in your early teenage years, but obviously you are fine now." They wondered what treatments he had received.

President Uchtdorf concluded, "it became clear to me that my regular exercise in fresh air as a laundry boy had been a key factor in my healing from this illness. Without the extra effort of pedaling that heavy bicycle day in and day out, pulling the laundry cart up and down the streets of our town, I might never have become a jet fighter pilot and later a 747 airline captain."[4]

I had a similar experience in my life. As a sophomore, I made the varsity basketball team and had the opportunity to make a real contribution. I made the varsity baseball team and made the starting lineup. At that point in my life, that was what was most important to me, so life was good. Then there was the girl situation. They were beginning to notice me, and I was definitely noticing them. Life was great. My sophomore year passed, and I had a wonderful summer and returned to school for my junior year full of anticipation for the year to come.

The year started out great. I went to homecoming with a great girl. Basketball season started, and I was in the starting lineup and we were a great team. Then it happened. My face began to break out a little bit. I was not too worried about it, but I decided to see a doctor anyway. The doctor prescribed me some medicine. Little did I know what would follow. My face broke out so badly I could hardly recognize myself. My skin dried out, and so did my muscles. I was getting injured a lot and sick even more. I lost my place in the starting lineup. Girls seemed not to recognize me anymore. I remember one night saying a prayer. I told God that if he could heal leprosy then surely he could handle acne. I begged for it to go away. I asked him to take it away that night as I was sleeping. I woke up the next morning, walked to the mirror, rubbed the sleep out of my eyes, turned on the light, and looked into the mirror. Tears ran down my face as I saw that my face looked worse than ever.

I remember looking at those who had clear skin and wishing I had it. I did not go to my junior prom, and friends who used to look up to me seemed to pity me. I felt so low.

Spring turned to summer and summer to fall. At some point in that process the medicine had done what it was designed to do, and I woke up and my face was clear. The trial was over. Girls began to notice me again, I had more confidence in myself, and everything seemed to settle back to normal with the exception of one thing that was changed forever: me. Looking back, that season of my life may have saved my life. It must have been heartbreaking to our Heavenly Father to watch one of his sons go through such a hard time, but not nearly as hard as it would have been to watch me forget everything that was important as I pursued everything that seemed important at the time.

I think of the story of Joseph of Egypt. His envious brothers threw him in a pit. Joseph must have been relieved and felt his prayers were answered when they pulled him out of the pit, but that relief must have turned quickly into despair when his brothers sold him as a slave. He became a slave to a man named Potiphar and worked hard to make the best of a bad situation. He was such a faithful servant that eventually he was put in charge of all that Potiphar had. Then he caught the attention of Potiphar's wife, who pressed him daily to lie with her. One day she became extremely forceful and grabbed him by his garment. He resisted the temptation and ran away. Potiphar's wife lied and said Joseph came on to her. Joseph was thrown in prison. He worked hard in prison and eventually was placed over the prison as well. The Pharaoh's baker and butler eventually joined him in prison, and he correctly interpreted their dreams with the request that the butler remember him and tell Pharaoh how he had been wronged. But the butler forgot Joseph.

I wish I had Joseph's journal from prison. He must have felt so low. I wonder if he ever felt as though God had forgotten him. Here he was, trying to be a good boy, and things just seemed to get worse and worse.

Two years after interpreting the dreams of the butler and the baker, Pharaoh had a disturbing dream. He saw seven fat cows consumed by seven sickly-looking cows. None of those around him could tell him the meaning of his dream. It was at this time that the butler finally remembered Joseph. Joseph was brought before Pharaoh and by the spirit of the Lord was able to interpret the dream. He told Pharaoh that there would be seven years of plenty followed by seven years of famine and that they should store food and supplies during the seven years of plenty to be consumed during the seven years of famine. Pharaoh appointed Joseph to oversee this effort, and Joseph did so, becoming second-in-command in Egypt and saving Egypt and his own family (the house of Israel) from the famine.

When it looked like Joseph's life was falling apart, it was actually falling into place. After his brothers had come to Egypt to get food and found out who Joseph was, they obviously felt awful for what they had done to him. Joseph responded by saying something that showed he understood the principles taught later by Paul in 2 Corinthians 4:17–18. He said to his brothers:

> Be not grieved, nor angry with yourselves, that ye sold me hither: for God did send me before you to preserve life. . . .
>
> And God sent me before you to preserve you a posterity in the earth, and to save your lives by a great deliverance.
>
> So now it was not you that sent me hither, but God. (Genesis 45:5, 7–8)

I am sure it was hard for God to watch Joseph suffer when he was trying to be so good. I am sure it was hard for Joseph to go through all of those hard experiences, and I am sure it will be hard for you to go through some of what you will have to experience in high school and beyond. But don't think that those trials are a sign that God does not care about you. Elder Jeffrey R. Holland taught:

> Everyone, including, and perhaps especially, the righteous, will be called upon to face trying times. When that happens we can sometimes fear that God has abandoned us, and we might be left, at least for a time, to wonder when our troubles will ever end. . . . Whenever these moments of our extremity come, we must not succumb to the fear that God has abandoned us or that He does not hear our prayers. He *does* hear us. He *does* see us. He *does* love us. When we are in dire circumstances and want to cry, "Where art Thou?" it is imperative that we remember He is right there with us—where He has always been! We must continue to believe, continue to have faith, continue to pray and plead with heaven, even if we feel for a time our prayers are not heard and that

God has somehow gone away. He *is* there. Our prayers *are* heard. And when we weep He and the angels of heaven weep with us.[5]

Life, especially teenage life, is really hard sometimes. But it is written that our "light affliction," which will last "but for a moment," will work for us a "far more exceeding and eternal weight of glory." May we turn our life over to God and know that even though sometimes he lets us "get shots," it is out of love.

Notes

1. Dallin H. Oaks, "The Challenge to Become," *Ensign*, Nov. 2000, 32–34.
2. Orson F. Whitney, quoted by Spencer W. Kimball in *Faith Precedes the Miracle* (Salt Lake City: Deseret Book, 1972), 98.
3. James E. Faust, "Where Do I Make My Stand?," *Ensign*, Nov. 2004, 18.
4. Dieter F. Uchtdorf, "See the End from the Beginning," *Ensign*, May 2006, 42–45.
5. Jeffrey R. Holland, "Lessons from Liberty Jail," *Ensign*, Sep. 2009, 26–33.

7 1 corinthians 2:9

TEMPTATION

To live for today with no regard for tomorrow or eternity.

IT IS WRITTEN

But as it is written, Eye hath not seen, nor ear heard, neither have entered into the heart of man, the things which God hath prepared for them that love him.

I WANT you to pause for a minute as you read this book and write something down. I want you to really think about the answer to three questions:

What is the most beautiful thing you have ever seen?

What is the most beautiful thing you have ever heard?

What is the best feeling you have ever had in your heart?

If you can imagine those things then you may be able to imagine how wonderful the doctrine of this verse is. If you were to imagine the most beautiful thing you have ever seen, heard, and felt and combine them into one experience, it would not be as wonderful as heaven. Nothing on this earth can compare to heaven.

Elder L. Tom Perry said:

> When we think of eternal life, what is the picture that comes to mind? I believe that if we could create in our minds a clear and true picture of eternal life, we would start behaving differently. We would not need to be prodded to do the many things involved with enduring to the end, like doing our home teaching or visiting teaching, attending our meetings, going to the temple, living moral lives, saying our prayers, or reading the scriptures. We would want to do all these things and more because we realize they will prepare us to go somewhere we yearn to go.[1]

The scriptures help us to get a picture of what eternal life is like. Doctrine and Covenants 130:2 teaches us that the "same sociality which exists among us here will exist among us there [in the celestial kingdom], only it will be coupled with eternal glory, which glory we do not now enjoy." What does that mean? It means that we are not just going to go to heaven and play the harp for eternity. We will have friends and family and still enjoy the wonderful associations we have in this life only it will be coupled with eternal glory.

Doctrine and Covenants 137 records a vision that Joseph Smith had of the celestial kingdom. He said:

> I saw the transcendent beauty of the gate through which the heirs of that kingdom will enter, which was like unto circling flames of fire;
>
> Also the blazing throne of God, whereon was seated the Father and the Son.
>
> I saw the beautiful streets of that kingdom, which had the appearance of being paved with gold. (vv. 2–4)

Doesn't the celestial kingdom sound beautiful?

In John 14:2 the Savior teaches that in his "Father's house there are many mansions. . . . I go to prepare a place for you." Revelation 21:4 teaches us that in the celestial glory "God shall wipe away all tears from their eyes; and there shall be no more death, neither sorrow, nor crying, neither shall there be any more pain."

What an amazing place the celestial kingdom is. Put together what the scriptures teach about that place: wonderful associations that last forever; awe-inspiring beauty; beautiful mansions; streets of gold; no death, crying, or pain.

There is great power in doing what Elder Perry suggested by having a picture of eternal life in our minds. Maybe an example can illustrate the power of having this picture in your mind. What if I were a multibillionaire who owned gold mines and I made a promise to you that if you graduated from high school without breaking the law of chastity or the Word of Wisdom I would give you one million dollars of gold as a reward. How tempted would you be if someone tried to entice you to break one of those two commandments?

Let's say you were at a party and someone walked up to you and offered you a beer and through their words or actions their message was, "if you drink this, you will be cool. You will fit in." If you are anything like me, I think your response would be something like, "Let's see here, I can drink this beer and have you think I am cool, or choose not to drink this beer and have a million dollars of gold. I will choose the million dollars."

What is gold in the next life? It is pavement! The cement in the celestial kingdom is so wonderful that we would be able to resist temptation easier here if it were offered to us.

Doctrine and Covenants 78:10 teaches us that "Satan seeketh to turn their hearts away from the truth, that they become blinded and understand not the things which are prepared for them." Why would Satan want to blind us so that we don't understand what is prepared for us? Because Satan has nothing to offer us that even comes close to what Heavenly Father has to offer us. He can't compete so all he can do is try to have us forget or not believe that the celestial kingdom is there. But it is there. I know it is.

Satan tries to get us to forget about forever and to focus on now. President Spencer W. Kimball said, "Whoever said that sin was not fun? Whoever claimed that Lucifer was not handsome, persuasive, easy, friendly? Sin is attractive and desirable. Transgression wears elegant gowns and sparkling apparel. It is highly perfumed; it has attractive features, a soft voice. It is found in educated circles and sophisticated groups. It provides sweet and comfortable luxuries. Sin is easy and has a big company of pleasant companions. It promises immunity from restrictions, temporary freedoms. It can momentarily satisfy hunger, thirst, desire, urges, passions, wants without immediately paying the price. But, it begins tiny and grows to monumental proportions—drop by drop, inch by inch"[2]

Sin may be attractive, desirable, and fun, and appear to be luxurious and sophisticated, but it is also temporary and hollow.

Late one night as I was traveling home from a speaking assignment, I stumbled upon a radio program. It was an episode of the Twilight Zone. In this episode three men had robbed a train in the middle of the desert and then hid themselves in a cave where they had invented a way to freeze themselves for a couple hundred years. They figured that by the time they woke up, people would have forgotten about the train robbery and the gold would be all theirs. Out of greed, two of the three were eventually killed, and the man left tried to haul the gold out of the desert. The program ended with the man collapsing on a road. A flying machine settled over him, and you heard the people talking about the poor plight of the man collapsed on the road. "What is he carrying in that sack?" one asked. "Pavement!" the other responded. These men had spent their whole time and effort trying to obtain something that was eventually of no value.

There is only one way to receive the riches of eternity, and that is through the Atonement of Jesus Christ. We access that Atonement through obedience to the principles and ordinances of the gospel. Everything we receive from sin is temporary.

When we are faced with moments in which we are tempted to forget about eternity and live for today, I hope we will always remember that it is written, "Eye hath not seen, nor ear heard, neither have entered into the heart of man, the things which God hath prepared for them that love him." As we remember this scripture and have an eternal perspective, I hope we will have the courage to resist the temptation, knowing that what is in store for those who do so is far greater than any short-term fun or pleasure the sin would provide.

Notes

1. L. Tom Perry, "The Gospel of Jesus Christ," *Ensign*, May 2008, 44.
2. Spencer W. Kimball, *Faith Precedes the Miracle* (Salt Lake City: Deseret Book, 1972), 229.

8 luke 9:24

TEMPTATION

To focus so much on yourself and on making yourself look good that you become self-centered and inconsiderate of others.

IT IS WRITTEN

For whosoever will save his life shall lose it: but whosoever will lose his life for my sake, the same shall save it.

AS you enter your high school years, you become a relatively independent person. You can do most of what you need to do on your own. High school is an important time, and the choices you make there have a big impact on what your future will be like. For example, in the ninth grade, your grades go on your official transcript, helping to determine what colleges will accept you. In the high school years, people outside of your immediate community begin to really notice you for athletics, and dreams of playing college sports either become more of a reality or seem to become unrealistic.

It is often during these years that voices mature and people begin to notice how beautiful you sing. Student government, with its inherent popularity and résumé-building possibilities, is on a larger scale than it was in junior high. It is usually in high school that we notice the opposite sex more. There are dances to invite others to and to hope to be asked to. We begin to realize what we like in the opposite sex and actually start to think of ending up with certain people and what it would be like to be married to them.

None of these things are bad things; in fact they are all very good. However, because these things have such a bearing on our future, if we are not careful, we can become so fixated upon ourselves and our own goals that we become self-centered. We can forget about those around us as we try to "find ourselves." The paradox here is that the Lord has taught that the way to find ourselves is to lose ourselves in the service of God and others.

President Thomas S. Monson said:

> The Savior taught His disciples, "For whosoever will save his life shall lose it: but whosoever will lose his life for my sake, the same shall save it" (Luke 9:24).
>
> I believe the Savior is telling us that unless we lose ourselves in service to others, there is little purpose to our own lives. Those who live only for themselves eventually shrivel up and figuratively lose their lives, while those who lose themselves in service to others grow and flourish—and in effect save their lives.[1]

President Spencer W. Kimball said that "in serving others, we 'find' ourselves. . . . The more we serve our fellowmen in appropriate ways, the more substance there is to our souls. We become more significant individuals as we serve others. . . . It is easier to 'find' ourselves because there is so much more of us to find!"[2]

I love those two quotes, and they are so applicable to high school life when you are trying to "find yourself." Obviously the Lord is not saying that we should be careless about developing our talents or doing our schoolwork or developing meaningful relationships with others. You will naturally have to spend a lot of time on yourself in high school, but it seems to me that you should be developing these talents with the intent to help and bless others. As you do so, you will realize your greatest potential. Because of the competitive nature of high school, the temptation might be to develop your talents to get noticed or to outdo other people and draw attention to yourself. If we live that way, we "shrivel up."

In the forty-sixth section of the Doctrine and Covenants, the Lord is speaking about spiritual gifts and why they are given to individuals in the Church. As I have read that section, some words or phrases have stuck out to me because they were mentioned over and over again.

> For verily I say unto you, they (spiritual gifts) are given for the benefit of those who love me and keep all my commandments, and him that seeketh so to do; that *all may be benefited*. . . .
>
> To some is given one, and to some is given another, that *all may be profited thereby*. . . .
>
> And again, it is given by the Holy Ghost to some to know the diversities of operations, whether they be of God, that the manifestations of the Spirit may be given to *every man to profit withal*. . . .
>
> To another is given the word of knowledge, that *all may be taught* to be wise and to have knowledge. . . .
>
> And all these gifts come from God, *for the benefit of the children of God*. . . .
>
> That unto some it may be given to have all those gifts, that there may be a head, in order that *every member*

may be profited thereby. (D&C 46:9, 12, 16, 18, 26, 29; emphasis added)

I have already mentioned the story of Samson and Delilah, but I think there is another lesson regarding Samson that is worth telling here. Prior to Samson's birth, the Israelites had been ruled by the Philistines for forty years. An angel appeared to Samson's mother, who had not been able to have children, and told her that she would have a son that would "begin to deliver Israel out of the hand of the Philistines" (Judges 13:5).

Samson was born with an extreme amount of strength. Early in his life he killed a young lion with his bare hands. It seems that one of Samson's problems was that he forgot why he was blessed with such great strength. He seemed to forget that his strength was given him to "begin to deliver Israel." Instead it seemed that he used his strength for his own purposes. He killed thirty Philistines and took their clothing and their bedding to pay off a debt he incurred when they figured out a riddle and in essence won a bet. When his father-in-law gave his wife to another man he decided to catch some foxes, light their tails on fire, and set them loose in the corn fields of the Philistines, burning them down. When the Philistines found out he had done so out of anger toward his father-in-law and wife, the Philistines had them killed. This enraged Samson more, and he smote them with a great slaughter (Judges 14–15). He died in one last fit of anger when he pulled down some pillars, collapsing a building upon himself and those who had gathered to mock him. I have been unable to find an instance in Samson's life where he used his great strength to help someone else. Because of this, his life "shriveled up."

I had an experience with my second daughter Ella that helped me understand how God may feel about us when we focus on using our gifts to help others. I went in for a parent-teacher conference with her kindergarten teacher. Her teacher told me that earlier that week she had asked the class who they knew who was nice and who liked to help others. As is common with kindergarten classes, all of the kids in the class raised their hands. The first boy said, "Ella." Her teacher told me that half of the class put down their hands and said, "He took mine." She went on to tell me how kind Ella was to the other kids in the class and said that she always tried to help kids who were having a bad day.

Her teacher could have said a lot of nice things about Ella that day that would have been wonderful to hear as her father. She could have told me that Ella was so athletic, artistic, or beautiful, and that would have been really nice. But none of those things would have meant as much to me as it did to hear that Ella was one who was recognized for being nice and helping others. Likewise, I think that we please our Heavenly Father when we use our talents to bless and lift others instead of trying to outdo others and lift up ourselves.

Do you use the talents God has blessed you with to lift and help others or to lift and help yourself? It is okay to want to excel; the problem sometimes lies in why we want to excel. I think that this topic is one of the greatest secrets for how to have a great high school experience. Forget about making yourself look good and try to make others feel good. As you do so, you will find yourself—your best self—and you will reach your full potential. When you are tempted to become self-centered, I hope that you will remember what is written:

"For whosoever will save his life shall lose it: but whoso-ever will lose his life for my sake, the same shall save it."

Notes

1. Thomas S. Monson, "What Have I Done for Someone Today?" *Ensign*, Nov. 2009, 85.
2. "President Kimball Speaks Out on Service to Others," *New Era*, Mar. 1981, 47.

9 matthew 6:33

TEMPTATION

To do so many good things that the most important things fall out of your life.

IT IS WRITTEN

But seek ye first the kingdom of God, and his righteousness; and all these things shall be added unto you.

HIGH school is a very busy time of life. You have school and homework, sports, choirs, bands, dance, and other extracurricular activities. You have church, seminary, Mutual, home teaching, presidency meetings, and BYC meetings. You have family home evening, temple attendance, scripture study, and prayer. Some of you hold down a part-time job to save for missions and college. Have you ever had this thought? "There is not enough time in the day to get done all that I need to get done." I would bet many of you have.

Well, to you and to busy people everywhere, the Savior has spoken clearly. He said, "seek you first the kingdom of God, and his righteousness; and all these things [the things that we worry about from day to day] shall be added to you."

Elder Richard G. Scott asked some soul-searching questions on this topic:

> Are there so many fascinating, exciting things to do or so many challenges pressing down upon you that it is hard to keep focused on that which is essential? When things of the world crowd in, all too often the wrong things take highest priority. Then it is easy to forget the fundamental purpose of life. Satan has a powerful tool to use against good people. It is distraction. He would have good people fill life with 'good things' so there is no room for the essential ones. Have you unconsciously been caught in that trap?[1]

In that same vein Elder Dallin H. Oaks gave a talk entitled "Good, Better, Best." He said that some things in life are good, others are better, but some are best, and we should make sure that we are making time for the best things in our lives. In that talk he said, "We should begin by recognizing the reality that just because something is *good* is not a sufficient reason for doing it. The number of good things we can do far exceeds the time available to accomplish them. Some things are better than good, and these are the things that should command priority attention in our lives."[2]

I have seen an object lesson done a couple of times that really impressed me. The person has a vase, and how much the vase holds represents the amount of time we have in our lives. They also have some golf balls (representing the "best" things that matter most in our lives), some marbles (representing the "better" things in our lives), and some sand (representing the "good" but nonessential things). They start by filling the vase with sand, then add the marbles, and then finally the golf balls. They measure each of those so that in the end there is not enough room for all of the golf balls.

They then empty the vase and repeat the process, except this time they put the golf balls in first, then the marbles, and then the sand. By doing this, all of the golf balls fit, all of the marbles fit, and most of the sand fits. I have seen some people do this where all of the sand fits. I don't think this is reality. I like it when some sand falls out of the vase. President Ezra Taft Benson said, "When we put God first, all other things fall into their proper place or drop out of our lives."[3] The truth of the matter is that you will not be able to do all of the good things you want to do. Some of those things may have to drop out of your lives.

I have met some youth who want to take seven AP classes, serve as student body officer, get a part-time job, play three sports, sing in the choir, play in the orchestra, become an Eagle Scout, and so on and so on. None of these things are bad; they are some of the "better" things that you could be doing with your life right now. But they are not the best things. Doing these things only becomes a problem when they prevent you from doing the "best things" in your life. If your schedule is too busy for scripture study, prayer, family home evening, church, attending the temple, seminary, and serving others, you are too busy.

One example of the many that came to mind is the choice whether or not to take seminary. The prophet has asked every young person to enroll in seminary. I have spoken with some teenagers who are frantically trying to get into a certain seminary class because that is all that would work for their schedule. We do all we can to accommodate them, but sometimes there is simply no way to do so. I have been impressed with the students and parents who, when faced with this situation, say, "Okay, I guess I will not be able to be in that choir or take that class I wanted to." They choose to obey the prophet and enroll in seminary and let something else fall out of their life. I have been saddened at times when parents or students give us the following ultimatum: "Let me (or let my child) in this class or I (they) will not take seminary." Many times their schedule is so tight because they are striving to excel in order to get into the college of their choice or take advantage of some other opportunity. I think that these moments are important moments to take a step back and ask ourselves if we really believe in the promise the Lord made in Matthew 6:33: "seek ye first the kingdom of God, and his righteousness; and all these things shall be added unto you."

Of all the things that will give you an advantage as you face the future, nothing will give you as big an advantage as having God on your side. You invite God into your life by putting him first in your life.

I remember a time when I faced a similar decision. I realized during my sophomore year of high school that I may have had an opportunity to play baseball beyond high school. I was being invited to play on some scout teams, and I had talked with a few scouts and received letters from a few colleges. I was very excited, and this became so important to me that the most important things took a backseat. My family and I were good people who loved the Church, the prophet, Joseph Smith, the Book of Mormon, and most important, Jesus Christ; however, I fear that during this portion of my life, I had filled my life with so many good things that I did not leave enough room for the best things.

I have always had a sensitive conscience. I feel really bad when I am involved in something wrong. I remember days when I was out playing ball on a Sunday when I would have a nagging pain in my heart because I knew I was not where I was supposed to be. For this and other reasons, I knelt down one evening late in the night to pray and ask Heavenly Father if I was okay and to find out what my standing was in his eyes. I had one of the strongest spiritual impressions that I have ever received that I should prepare to serve a mission. I had just signed my letter of intent to play baseball at Cal State Los Angeles. After talking with my father, I decided to honor the commitment I had made to Cal State LA for my freshman year and then prepare to serve a mission.

I also had a few other experiences growing up that left an indelible impression on me and contributed greatly to my serving a mission. My older brother Shawn always wanted to attend seminary. I was always worried about it making me too tired for sports because we had to wake up early and go to the church before school. I went because Shawn went. One day in seminary we watched a movie titled *Called to Serve*. That is the first time I ever remember feeling a desire to serve a mission, and that has stuck with me to this day. I also had attended my cousin Chad Martin's farewell in June, after my graduation, and was touched by what happened there that day, which strengthened my resolve to serve a mission. Maybe most of all, I had been very much impressed by the temple marriage of my brother Shane a few years prior to this. I remember a talk we had in the backyard one time when he talked about how hard a mission was but how big of an impact it had had in his life. I even remember to this day what the weather was like and that we were swinging golf clubs. I felt the Spirit that day, and I remember referring back to that experience a few times when I was getting off track. I wanted what Shane had: a beautiful wife who he was sealed to forever and a confidence that he was doing the will of the Lord. I remember how proud I was of him as we unpacked his big storage chest the day he got home from his mission. He was bigger than life to me. All of these things went through my mind at one time or another during my time preparing for a mission.

I enrolled in and began attending Cal State LA in the fall of 1995. The adversary instantly began to work on me through peer pressure, girls, and pride. I was constantly surrounded by temptations. It was really hard to hold on to those spiritual experiences I had experienced, and sometimes it was really hard to feel the Spirit in that environment.

I went home for Christmas—we had almost a month break—and it felt so good to be home and not surrounded by so many temptations. I made some resolutions that I thought would help me live in the world and not be affected by it so much. I made commitments to read my scriptures and pray.

The season began, and I was not in the starting lineup our first game. At first I was a little relieved because that would make it easier to leave baseball behind. But that relief, if you could call it that, was short lived. Our third baseman struck out looking at a called third strike in the first inning and threw his bat in disgust at the umpire's call. My coach, an old war vet and Stanford graduate named John Herbold III, told him to stop pouting and take a seat. "If it's close enough to call a strike, you should be good enough to hit it" was his philosophy, and he had zero tolerance for blaming our mistakes on the umpire or anyone else. He sat down the third baseman and yelled to me, "Marty, go to third and take this whiner's spot." I ran into the game, and the first pitch was hit to me. I fielded it cleanly and made the play, which calmed my nerves. When I came up to bat the first time, I hit a hard line drive to the shortstop. This induced some praise from my coach, who yelled to the rest of the team, "He's a freshman, and he can hit. Some of you stinkin' seniors need to take some notes." The rest of the day was great. I got hits in my next two at-bats, and I stole three bases. I never left the lineup for the rest of the year.

I began to concentrate a lot on baseball again—probably too much. During this time I was reading in my Book of Mormon one evening. Some bad things were going on in the other room, and I went into my bedroom to escape it. As I read the Book of Mormon, I felt something that I had never felt so dramatically before. I felt calm, at home, strengthened, and peaceful. I knelt down, thanked Heavenly Father for that feeling, and asked if I could continue to feel it. As I was praying, I heard someone walk into the room. I wondered if I would be made fun of. I was still on my knees, but I had stopped praying and started to plan a speech in my head about respecting my beliefs. After waiting a few minutes in vain for someone to make fun of me, I said another little prayer of thanks and sat up on my bed. It turned out that I had underestimated my roommate's level of respect for sacred things. He was standing in my doorway watching me the whole time. He said, "Hey, if

I leave, will you say one of those for me?" I told him that he could pray for himself. He said, "My life is messed up right now. You are a good guy. God will listen to you. Please, say a prayer for me." I agreed to do so. He came back in a few minutes and made sure I had done so, and we talked on the bed about his life until late into the night.

This had a profound effect on me. It was my first missionary experience. Also, I looked up to this person a lot. He was a good baseball player who had been drafted straight out of high school but chose to forgo the minor leagues to play college ball and get an education. He was a ladies' man and well-liked by all who knew him. He had a great heart and, even though he did not share my beliefs, he had a sincerity about him. He had everything that I was working for, yet there he was, sitting on my bed and asking me about how his life could be better. I realized that day how fortunate I was to know what I know. From that day on, he made it so much easier for me to live how I wanted to live. The enticements to do bad things ceased after that experience. I was able to read my Book of Mormon on road trips without being bothered. I gained respect from my teammates.

One day while in Northern California playing Stanford and University of San Francisco, we went over the Golden Gate Bridge as a team to a lookout point where you could see the San Francisco skyline. On the way back over, two of my friends on the team called me to the back of the bus. One of them said, "Hey, you are a good Mormon." I said, "Thank you. You are a good baseball player." He continued, "We both have friends who are Mormon, and those who live it leave on missions when they are nineteen. Are you going to keep living it?" This was an interesting question. I was beginning to be tempted not to serve a mission because of the success I was having on the baseball field and the attention I was getting from some scouts. As I sat there on the bus, I kept thinking, "I have to serve a mission. It is what God wants me to do. I will never go wrong doing what he wants me to do. He will take care of me." I told my teammate that I was going to serve a mission. This is the moment when I felt like my decision was solidified. I never remember questioning again whether or not I would serve a mission.

When the day came to tell my coach I was leaving on a mission, I was very nervous. He was a grumpy old man at times and had even been known to throw things at his players on occasion. I also was afraid of offending him. He is now in the College Coaches Hall of Fame, and he had a lot of pull in the baseball world. He was a good man to have on your side if you wanted to play professional baseball, which I did. I was fasting that morning and prayed for strength. A number of my teammates went with me to tell my coach. I walked into his office and said, "Coach, I am a member of The Church of Jesus Christ of Latter-day Saints and—" He interrupted and finished my sentence, "You are going on a mission." I said, "Yes." "Water my plant," he said as he handed me a plant and an old coke can and pointed to the door. My teammates were leaning up against the door trying to hear the coach's reaction. You should have seen the look on their faces when I walked out with a plant in my hand. I watered the plant and went back in to see my coach. He said, "Well, there are very few things in this life more important than baseball, and God might be one of them." I said, "To me he is,

Coach." We parted ways on friendly terms. He even wrote me a few letters on my mission.

I can share my personal testimony with you that there *are* some things in life more important than baseball, choir, AP classes, college, and many of the other good things we have the opportunity to do. Everything that I have in my life right now I can connect to that opportunity I had to serve a mission. I put God first in that situation, and I have seen his hand in my life ever since. I know that he will take care of you if you put him first in your life as well.

When you are tempted to fill your life so full of good things that there is no room for the essential things, I hope you will remember that it is written, "Seek ye first the kingdom of God, and his righteousness; and all these things shall be added unto you." The Savior will keep his promise. I have seen it in my own life.

Notes

1. Richard G. Scott, "First Things First," *Ensign*, May 2001, 6.
2. Dallin H. Oaks, "Good, Better, Best," *Ensign*, Nov. 2007, 104–8.
3. Ezra Taft Benson, "The Great Commandment—Love the Lord," *Ensign*, May 1988, 4.

10 d+c 58:42-43

TEMPTATION

To hide your sins because you are afraid or embarrassed to confess them.

IT IS WRITTEN

Behold, he who has repented of his sins, the same is forgiven, and I, the Lord, remember them no more.

By this ye may know if a man repenteth of his sins—behold, he will confess them and forsake them.

IN addressing the scenario above, I would first like to say that all of us should feel very grateful for guilt. Guilt is to our spirit like physical pain is to our body. We do not want to get to the point in life that we are "past feeling" guilt when we do something wrong. That is where Laman and Lemuel were when Nephi said of them, "Ye are swift to do iniquity but slow to remember the Lord your God. Ye have seen an angel, and he spake unto you; yea, ye have heard his voice from time to time; and he hath spoken unto you in a still small voice, but *ye were past feeling*, that ye could not feel his words" (1 Nephi 17:45; emphasis added).

I was intrigued by an article that I read a while back about a girl who had a rare disease that made her body incapable of feeling pain. That might sound awesome to us. What would life be like if our bodies felt no pain? Well, for this little girl it was hard. The article told of how the little girl has to have ice in her chili to cool it down, otherwise she would gulp it down not realizing that she was scolding her throat and stomach. She would chew her tongue while eating and not know it, and when she had an infection without any outward symptoms it would take longer than normal to find and treat it. I was especially intrigued by this statement from her mother, "Some people would say that's a good thing. But no, it's not. Pain's there for a reason. It lets your body know something's wrong and it needs to be fixed. I'd give anything for her to feel pain."[1] Some would also think that never feeling guilty would be a good thing, but it is not. Guilt is there to let your soul know that something is wrong spiritually and that something needs to be fixed.

So what do we do when we feel guilt? We don't run away from the very things that will help us get better. We do what Doctrine and Covenants 58 teaches us to do: we repent by confessing and forsaking our sins.

I have had many meetings with youth in which this subject has come up. When I ask them what it is about repentance that makes it hard to do, they almost universally talk about the embarrassment of confessing the sin. I know many youth who have forsaken the sin but have not gotten up the courage to confess it, especially when that confession involves speaking to a priesthood leader. They carry a weight that is unbearable and a guilt that is not necessary.

I assume many of you have been on a long hike before where you have had to carry a backpack. My cousin Chad and I go on a long backpacking and fly-fishing trip each summer. One summer we decided to hike the Wind River Mountains in Wyoming. Our plan was to hike until we saw a mountain lake. Then we would hike down to the lake to fish and then back up again on the way to our final destination. By the time we got to our final campsite, we were completely exhausted. We were hot, sweaty, and covered in bug spray. My muscles were so tired that my legs were shaking. Those who have experienced this know how exhilarating it feels to finally drop that backpack and be relieved of the weight of it. I can still remember how good it felt to unlatch the straps of my backpack, feel that weight coming off of my shoulders, and feel the wind blow across the sweaty spots on my shirt where the straps had been. I remember how good it felt as we got in our swim trunks and walked to a little waterfall that emptied into a water hole. We dove in and soaked our sore muscles in the cool, refreshing water.

My young friends, spiritually speaking, some of you are carrying a backpack with you everywhere you go. You probably do not realize how much of a burden you are carrying. You have forgotten what it feels like to walk without your "backpack of guilt." You have forgotten what it feels like to sit in a church meeting or seminary or a youth conference and to feel good, pure, and peaceful. The Lord is inviting us in Doctrine and Covenants 58:42–43 to take off the backpack and wash ourselves. Elder Scott gave this invitation to those who feel guilty: "If you have a troubled conscience from broken laws, I plead, please come back. Come back to the cool, refreshing waters of personal purity. Come back to the warmth and security of Father in Heaven's love. Come back to the serenity and peace of conscience that come from living the commandments of God."[2]

One of my favorite parables the Savior taught is the parable of the prodigal son. I have already mentioned this parable once in this book, but I want to emphasize a different part of the story here. By way of review, a younger son asks for his inheritance and then goes off and wastes it in riotous and sinful ways. The young man's life becomes so rough that he is staring at some pigs he has been hired to take care of and envies them because they have slop to eat, and he wishes he could eat the slop. Eventually the scriptures say "he came to himself" and decided to return to his father. He did not feel worthy to be his son but thought at least he could be his servant and have food to eat.

I want to pause here to point something out about the rest of this story. It is important for us to realize that this is the Savior telling this parable. He is using this story to teach us how he and his Father react when we come to ourselves, decide that we are tired of living a sinful life, and want to return to them.

The young man approaches his home, and he was "yet a great way off" when his father saw him. This suggests that the father had been looking for him. His father ran to him, fell on his neck, and kissed him. He brought forth the best robe and put it on his son, put a ring on his finger, and placed shoes on his feet. He then prepared a feast and had a party because his son who was dead and lost was now alive and found.

What does this parable teach us about how the Savior reacts when we come to him and ask for forgiveness? He runs to us to help us through it and rewards us. Some of you seem to think that you cannot be forgiven because you knew what you were doing was wrong when you did it. Of course you did. That is the definition of sin. That is the very thing we need to be saved from. So did this young man when he went off and wasted his inheritance. The beautiful message of this parable is that when we come to ourselves and want to return to God, he is there and eagerly waiting our return.

So how do we return? That is the message of D&C 58:42–43. We confess our sins and then we forsake them. As we do so, the Lord gives us the wonderful promise that he will remember them no more. What a wonderful blessing. I know that the Savior really does forgive us of our sins and does not remember them when we repent. Elder Richard G. Scott said, "I testify that when a bishop or stake president has confirmed that your repentance is sufficient, know that your obedience has allowed the Atonement of Jesus Christ to satisfy the demands of justice for the laws you have broken. Therefore you are now free. Please believe it."[3]

Notes

1. "Rare disease makes girl unable to feel pain," MSNBC.com, Nov. 1, 2004, http://www.msnbc.msn.com/id/6379795/ns /health-childrens_health/t/rare-disease-makes-girl-unable -feel-pain/.
2. Richard G. Scott, "Peace of Conscience and Peace of Mind," *Ensign*, Nov. 2004, 15–18.
3. Ibid.

conclusion

IN the first chapter of the book of Joshua, Joshua is called to succeed Moses. He would be the one to lead the children of Israel into the promised land. He would be the one to lead them in battle against the giant Amorites. What a daunting responsibility that would have been. He may have felt a lot like you when you face the daunting tasks associated with high school.

Under this extreme pressure, the Lord gave him counsel to comfort his heart:

"This book of the law [the scriptures] shall not depart out of thy mouth; but thou shalt meditate therein day and night, that thou mayest observe to do according to all that is written therein: for then thou shalt make thy way prosperous, and then thou shalt have good success" (Joshua 1:8). I believe that, like Joshua, if you will meditate upon and observe to do according to all that is written in the scriptures, you will be prosperous and have good success in high school and beyond.

By way of review:

When you are tempted to hang out with a friend or a group of friends even if they are a bad influence on you, I hope you will remember what is written in Matthew 18:8–9.

When you are tempted to think the Church is restrictive and that life would be so much more fun without all of the Church's rules, I hope that you will remember what is written in Mosiah 2:41.

When you are tempted to do something that you know is wrong to fit in with or to impress someone else, I hope you will remember what is written in James 1:14–15.

When you are tempted to not say your prayers, either out of laziness or because you feel guilty for something you have done, I hope you will remember what is written in 2 Nephi 32:8–9.

When you are tempted to not like yourself and to wish you were somebody else, I hope you will remember what is written in Alma 29:1–3.

When you are tempted to feel that God must not care about you because of the trials you are experiencing, I hope you will remember what is written in 2 Corinthians 2:17–18.

When you are tempted to live for today with no regard for tomorrow or eternity, I hope you will remember what is written in 1 Corinthians 2:9.

When you face the temptation to focus so much on yourself and making yourself look good that you become self-centered and inconsiderate of others, I hope you will remember what is written in Luke 9:24.

When you are tempted to do so many good things that the most important things fall out of your life, I hope you will remember what is written in Matthew 6:33.

When you are tempted to hide your sins because you are afraid or embarrassed to confess them, I hope you will remember what is written in D&C 58:42–43.

I hope that each of you can follow the example of Joseph Smith, Moses, and of course the Savior, Jesus Christ, and resist the temptations of the adversary by remembering what is written and, like them, go on to achieve your full potential and accomplish all the wonderful things you are supposed to accomplish in this life.